Tableside Cookery

Tableside Cookery

Sergio Andrioli
and
Peter Douglas

VNR VAN NOSTRAND REINHOLD
New York

Copyright © 1990 by Sergio Andrioli and Peter Douglas

Library of Congress Catalog Card Number 89-21511
ISBN 0-442-30309-2

Published in the United States of America by
Van Nostrand Reinhold
115 Fifth Avenue
New York, New York 10003

Distributed in Canada by
Nelson Canada
1120 Birchmount Road,
Scarborough, Ontario MlK 5G4, Canada

16 15 14 13 12 11 10 9 8 7 6 5 4 3 2 1

Library of Congress Cataloging-in-Publication Data
Andrioli, Sergio.
    Tableside Cookery/Sergio Andrioli and Peter Douglas.
        p.   cm.
    ISBN 0−442−30309−2
    1. Chafing dish cookery.   I. Douglas, Peter (Peter Jeffrey)
II. Title.
TX825.A54   1990   89-21511
641.5′8-dc20   CIP
Made and printed in Spain by Printeksa, Bilbao

◆ *Contents* ◆

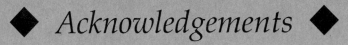

We wish to thank: David Terry, Principal, and Nic Bailey, Head of the Faculty of Catering, Halesowen College, for allowing us to use the college's facilities, and for their encouragement; our colleagues for their support; Rosalyn Myatt and the technicians for their help.

We would also like to thank: Steward Smith, manager of the *Plough and Harrow*, Birmingham, for allowing us to use his establishment's facilities.

Our special thanks to: Giovanni Divito, the sous chef, for the help and assistance he gave us during the photographic sessions; Andy Knock, who was responsible for the photography; Peter Swann, who was responsible for the drawings; and, finally, Mr Blacklock of the CGLI, for his initial support.

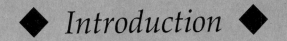

Introduction

This book is a practical guide for students preparing for examinations in advanced food service.

It is also recommended reading for students on other courses in hotel and catering operations because it will give them a clear idea of the principles and the main skills involved in advanced food service, and the practical application of the various techniques required in this type of work. In addition, this book will prove beneficial to food service lecturers and all those involved in the teaching of this style of service.

The names of all the dishes shown in this book are given in both French and English, but some of the technical terms in the text are in French only.

A glossary of culinary terms with short explanations can be found at the end of Chapter 6, thus making long, detailed, repetitive explanations in the text unnecessary.

All weights and measures are given in metric and Imperial amounts. However, it should be noted that the amounts given in the recipes relate to ratio formulas and do not relate to each other. Therefore, 1 oz may equate with 25 g or 30 g, depending upon the dish in question.

Sergio Andrioli and Peter Douglas

CHAPTER ONE

◆ *Guéridon service* ◆

SECTION ONE
History and development of guéridon service

SECTION TWO
Advantages and disadvantages of guéridon service

SECTION THREE
Organization of service

SECTION FOUR
Behaviour and deportment

Since its introduction from Russia in the nineteenth century, this style of service has played an important role in the catering industry, especially the high-class sector.

It was formerly known as 'Russian service' and involved the service of large joints, poultry, game and fish, all of which were elaborately decorated. The food was displayed on a sideboard or on side tables. It was presented carved or portioned by service staff and customers had as much or as little as they required.

Since its introduction, the style of service evolved and underwent several changes. Parts of the original service are used today and can be seen in the form of a cold carving buffet or guéridon service, where the food is prepared and served from a side table.

The French word 'guéridon' means a round table from which food is prepared, carved, finished and served. During the nineteenth century, guéridon service became more and more popular, especially in the more exclusive establishments. By the beginning of the century it was well-established as the most fashionable way of serving food.

An important innovation, and an extension of this style of service, was the introduction of flambé work by Henri Charpentier, who when working as a commis de rang at the *Cafe de Paris*, Monte Carlo, seized the opportunity to prepare a pancake dish of his creation for a party hosted by Edward, Prince of Wales. During the preparation, the dish was accidentally set alight when the spirit was added to it, much to the delight of the important guests.

According to Henri Charpentier the dish was a success and was named crêpes suzette at the request of the Prince of Wales himself. The incident marked the beginning of a new trend. In the years that followed flambé work became widespread.

Guéridon service has always been associated with exclusive catering establishments offering an extensive à la carte menu. It must be appreciated, however, that this style of service can be adapted to suit lesser establishments offering a more restricted choice of menu and can be operated to complement other styles of service.

In recent years the presentation of food for service has been affected by the introduction of nouvelle cuisine. This involves the dishes being delicately presented on a plate using intricate designs, the theme being to concentrate on colour, texture and taste. The effect on the restaurant is that less skilled staff are required.

The most recent development, cuisine naturelle, has come about because of the awareness of the benefits of healthy eating. The food is cooked with a minimum of cream, butter, etc. and the idea is to use the natural flavours of the ingredients to complement one another. The style of service is similar to that of nouvelle cuisine, again minimizing the need for skilled staff.

Although some establishments have adopted these styles of food preparation and service there are still many hotels and restaurants using the classical guéridon service. It is interesting to note that although the guéridon style is more expensive to implement than other forms of service the menu prices in comparable establishments do not show a marked variation.

A big criticism of the nouvelle and naturelle cuisine is that the size of portions are small and do not give sufficient value for money.

Advantages and disadvantages of guéridon service

The use of this form of service affords both the customer and the caterer many advantages but there are a few disadvantages:

◆ Advantages

- ◆ The customer receives a more personalized style of service with individual attention.
- ◆ The customer enjoys the benefit of a more varied choice on the menu.
- ◆ The food is freshly prepared and, in the case of flambé dishes, cooked to order.
- ◆ The standard of hygiene is high because of the close proximity of the waiter to the customer.
- ◆ The quality of food has to match the quality of service.
- ◆ The customer is given the facility to state any preferences he or she may have in the preparation of a particular dish.
- ◆ In the hands of an experienced member of staff, the preparation of many dishes can be entertaining.
- ◆ The service is carried out at a more leisurely pace giving the customer time to enjoy the meal experience.

- ◆ This style of service helps an establishment to promote itself, therefore maximizing sales.
- ◆ Staff achieve job satisfaction, thus improving motivation and reducing staff turnover.
- ◆ Guéridon service has a definite influence on the standard grading of an establishment in the eyes of a customer.
- ◆ Customers are more pampered since establishments using this style of service are more interested in quality than quantity.

◆ Disadvantages

- ◆ The initial cost of buying specialist equipment for this style of service can be high but good profit margins can still be obtained by the skilled restaurateur.
- ◆ Finding suitably skilled members of staff to carry out this style of service can be a problem.
- ◆ Labour costs can be high but this can be offset by the extra income generated by their skills.

In order to achieve and maintain a satisfactory standard of service, certain rules and procedures should be adhered to.

Before service begins the station waiter should always prepare his or her guéridon for service as part of the mise-en-place.

The guéridon should be covered with a clean cloth, stocked with service spoons and forks, and any other equipment required. This will depend upon the tasks to be carried out. The guéridon should be placed in position before any food arrives from the kitchen. In order to minimize accidents, the guéridon should always be pushed, *never pulled*, since the waiter cannot see where he or she is going while walking backwards.

The guéridon should be placed as near to the table being served as is safely possible. This will enable the guest to have a clear view of the work being carried out. The waiter should always face the customer and never obstruct the customer's view of the guéridon.

During the service, when the food is required, the commis waiter should always take the dishes to the sideboard first then, depending on priority, one dish at a time should be placed on the guéridon.

All dishes requiring portioning, preparation or finishing at the table should be presented to the customer beforehand. The reasons for presenting the dishes are as follows:

◆ To ensure that the correct dish is being served.
◆ In the case of a dish being assembled, finished or cooked at the table, the customer would have the opportunity to state his or her preference, that is, the customer may only ask for the head and tail of a trout to be removed or may request that a certain ingredient be omitted from a particular dish.
◆ It will enable the customer to see and appreciate the artistic skills of the chefs in the presentation of the dishes.

Figure 1 *A guéridon ready for service*

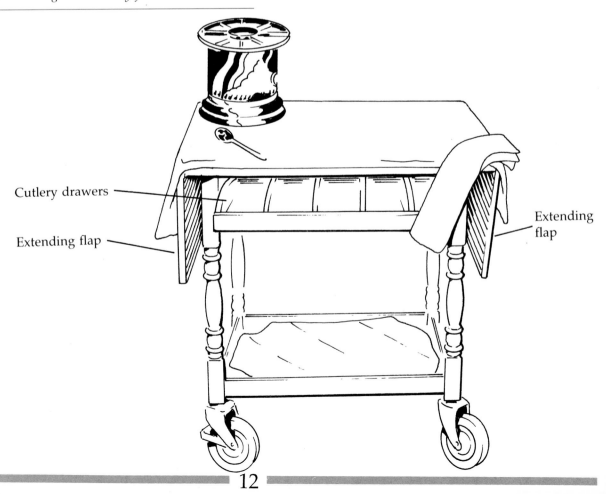

Cutlery drawers

Extending flap

Extending flap

When placing any dishes on a rechaud or a flare lamp, the station waiter should remove the underflat in order to allow maximum heat penetration. China dishes should not be placed on flare lamps unless they are flameproof.

When transferring food from the dish to the plate the waiter should hold the service spoon and fork in separate hands and, in order to prevent any sauce from dripping over the guéridon or the edge of the plate, the fork should be run underneath the spoon. Any drops of sauce marring the appearance of the food on the plate should be wiped with a clean service cloth.

The plate with the food on it should then be handed to the commis waiter who will place it in front of the customer from the right. (The station waiter should instruct the commis waiter as to which customer the food is intended for.)

In the case of a main course, vegetables are usually silver served either on the main course plate or on a separate plate placed on the left-hand side of the cover. Sauces and accompaniments can either be served at the guéridon or at the table. It is essential that any food served should be at the correct temperature when it reaches the customer and, in the case of hot food, it should be piping hot.

When serving a mixed party whenever possible ladies should be served first. However, in the case where a lady and a gentleman are having the same dish it is acceptable to serve them both before any other lady in the party.

When cooking at the table, before starting, the guéridon should be moved back in order to create a safe gap between the trolley and the customer.

If a certain dish requires a lengthy guéridon preparation, the station waiter should not send for the remainder of the order until the dish is near completion. Timing is crucial in this case.

The waiter should take great care when setting a dish alight with spirit. Too big a flame could be dangerous and cause the customer some distress. However, too small a flame or if no flame at all was produced it would be an anticlimax and disappoint the customer. This is where training and practice are essential in order to acquire the necessary skills and instinctive judgement to carry out the task safely and effectively.

When transferring the finished dish to the plate the pan should be rested on a joint plate to prevent it burning the trolley cloth.

The flare lamp can also be used for keeping food hot and for reheating.

When the service of a particular course at a table is finished, the guéridon should be cleared of dirties, cleaned and made ready for the next table or course. If necessary, the cloth should be turned or changed.

◆ Conversing with customers

The waiter or waitress must be able to converse with customers in a clear and concise manner. Although a customer may welcome snippets of conversation on the procedures being carried out at the guéridon, great care should be taken to ensure that this should not become overpowering.

◆ Mannerism

Restaurant personnel should display an impeccable manner during service and all work carried out should be done with flair, panache and dexterity.

◆ Selling

It must not be forgotten that the main duty of a waiter or waitress is to sell. However, this should be done softly in the form of suggestions rather than 'hard sell' tactics. The proper training of staff is essential if a satisfactory standard is to be achieved. This should include how to maximize existing sales.

◆ Anticipation of customers' needs

A very observant person will be able to anticipate some customers' requests before they are formulated. This is when a good waiter can show his or her professional know-how and realize sales which would otherwise have been lost.

CHAPTER TWO

◆ *Health and safety* ◆

SECTION ONE
Personal hygiene and appearance

SECTION TWO
Hygienic working practices

SECTION THREE
Safety and accident prevention

SECTION FOUR
Legal aspects

The standard of dress and personal hygiene of waiters and waitresses must be very high because of the nature of guéridon service requiring them to work in close proximity to customers for long periods of time.

All restaurant personnel should wash regularly and should pay particular attention to the following:

◆ Hair

Hair should be kept clean and tidy. It should be well-groomed and styled in such a manner as to avoid contact with the face. Waitresses with long hair should tie it back or up, away from their face. Waiters should keep the length of their hair above the shirt collar.

Regular shampooing is essential to prevent dandruff (most uniforms are black so dandruff would be noticeable and spoil their appearance).

◆ Face

Waiters should be clean-shaven. A neat moustache is tolerated, but it is not recommended even though facial hair is becoming more socially acceptable. In our experience people with moustaches or beards have a habit of frequently touching or scratching their faces, which can cause the transfer of bacteria or viruses from their hands to the food.

◆ Teeth

Teeth should be brushed regularly and kept clean. Bad breath should be kept under control by using breath fresheners, etc.

◆ Hands

Hands must be washed frequently and special attention should be paid to *always* washing hands after a visit to the toilet.

Nails should be kept clean, short and well-groomed.

◆ Feet

The proper care of feet is vital. They must be washed regularly and toenails kept trimmed.

◆ The use of cosmetics

The use of make-up is tolerated but it must be kept to a minimum.

Deodorants, although recommended, must not be strong smelling (unperfumed ones are available) and perfumes should not be used at all.

Nail varnish chips off and becomes unsightly very quickly so, therefore, it is unacceptable.

◆ Uniforms

Uniforms are used to differentiate between members of staff and to ensure that no outdoor clothes are worn by restaurant personnel when serving food. Uniforms are often used to complement a specific theme within a restaurant. If properly designed they not only enhance the waiter's appearance but give a feeling of self-respect and an air of professionalism (if you look the part you feel the part).

To meet general and personal hygiene requirements, uniforms should be tailored, regularly laundered, kept in a good state of repair and regularly changed.

Socks, tights or stockings should be changed at least once a day and they must complement the uniform.

Comfortable shoes are essential. High-heeled shoes are not recommended. Whenever possible, shoes chosen should have leather soles which allow the feet to breathe. All shoes should be well-polished and kept in a good state of repair.

◆ Jewellery

The only acceptable piece of jewellery is a wedding ring. However, restaurant personnel may wear a watch in order to aid them during service.

In order to avoid the transfer of bacteria from a waiter's hands to a customer's plate, food should not be eaten during service. The picking of food is a particularly bad habit.

The chewing of gum is to be discouraged because:

◆ It favours the transfer of bacteria.
◆ It makes conversation difficult.

Cigarette smoking by waiters during service will also cause the transfer of bacteria from the mouth to the hands and customers may find the smell of stale smoke on the waiter's breath offensive.

Waiters and waitresses should always carry a clean handkerchief and use it to cover their face if they have to cough or sneeze. They must always turn away from the food and customers. Blowing of the nose should always be done out of the service area. In all of these cases waiters and waitresses should remember to wash their hands.

The service cloth should always be clean and, it should be if necessary, changed frequently during service.

Any cuts or sores must be covered with a clean dressing.

When a piece of cutlery is dropped on the floor, the waiter or waitress should immediately replace it with a clean piece before retrieving the soiled one. This ensures that customers are not given the impression that they have received the soiled piece of cutlery back.

If a waiter drops a dish containing food in the restaurant he should immediately order a replacement before clearing the food from the floor and placing it on his sideboard. The new portion of food should be served as soon as possible. The soiled food can then be removed from the restaurant and disposed of.

Accidents in the restaurant can be prevented. The following safety procedures should be observed.

◆ Care and maintenance of equipment

A flare lamp should not only be kept clean but it must also be filled to the correct level with methylated spirits or, in the case of a gas lamp, the cannister must be fitted securely to ensure that no leaks take place.

After dismantling the lamp for cleaning, care should be taken to ensure that:

◆ The burner is securely tightened down.
◆ The outer casing is correctly fitted.
◆ The top on which the pan rests is level.

Suzette pans should be regularly polished, inside and out, and washed thoroughly to remove all traces of the polish, which could taint the food. The silver lining of the pan must not be allowed to wear down to the copper layer because copper poisoning could result.

◆ Training

All restaurant personnel should have proper training in the use of equipment. It is recommended that regular refresher courses are implemented. This would ensure that all new members of staff were made familiar with the working practices of an establishment.

◆ Working environment

Adequate space should be allowed between tables in order to facilitate the movement of guéridon trolleys and staff.

Any defects in the carpet or floor covering should be reported immediately and all staff made aware of the danger.

All power points should be inspected regularly and staff prevented from using any that are faulty.

◆ Movement of staff

◆ On no account should staff run in the restaurant.
◆ Staff should pass each other on the right to avoid confusion and congestion.
◆ A waiter dropping any item of equipment while moving through the restaurant should not suddenly stop to pick it up as this could cause a collision. The waiter should return to retrieve the object as soon as possible.
◆ The correct service doors should always be used when entering and leaving the restaurant. A waiter should walk forward through the door having opened it first with his foot (that is, he should not walk backwards through the door).

◆ Human factors

The consumption of alcohol by staff when on duty should not be allowed because it will impair their judgement and affect their efficiency.

Staff should be given the correct breaks in order to ensure that they are not overtired. A member of staff suffering from fatigue is less efficient and more prone to carelessness.

Legislation on health and safety and food hygiene is summarized from *Beverage Sales and Service* by Brian Julyan (Heinemann Professional Publishing, 1988) as follows:

◆ Health and safety at work etc. Act 1974

The Health and Safety at Work Act etc. 1974, as amended by the Fire Precaution Act 1971, in effect makes it obligatory for any premises used for the sale of food and drink to obtain a fire certificate.

The employer (hereafter referred to as 'He') must take reasonable precautions to ensure the employees' health, safety and welfare as far as is reasonably practical while they are at work.

He must provide a safe place of work and take all reasonable precautions to see that it remains safe. He must also ensure the health and safety of customers and guests as far as is reasonably practical. This includes the safe structure of the building, electrical and gas installations, safe floor and stairs coverings (for example, no frayed or turned-up carpet edges) and dry uncluttered floors. All fire and emergency exits must be kept clear.

The employer must provide equipment which is safe when used correctly and which must be correctly installed and maintained. He must provide adequate training for staff so that they know the correct methods and techniques of using the equipment.

He must provide safe methods of access to all rooms.

In establishments with more than five employees, the employer must provide a written health and safety policy which is shown to the employees.

A record must be kept of any accident to an employee causing him to be unable to work for three or more days. Serious accidents or occurrences regarding dangerous situations must be reported to the environmental health officer immediately. All accidents to employees which occur at their place of work must by law be recorded. A standard accident book is available from HMSO.

Although the employer is held responsible for any act of negligence causing loss or injury to a customer, an employee must exercise reasonable care and skill in the performance of his duties and could be held liable for any loss or injury to a customer. The employee must safeguard the health and safety or colleagues as well as self.

No person shall intentionally or recklessly interfere with or misuse anything provided in the interests of health, safety or welfare.

◆ Offices, Shops and Railways Premises Act 1963

This Act covers persons employed in the sales and service of beverages in hotels and restaurants, but excludes employees of registered clubs and purely residential hotels.

It requires that the work and public areas are kept clean, clear and well lit. Non-public work areas must be kept at a minimum of 16°C.

Drinking water and cups, or a drinking fountain, must be available for employees. Sufficient toilets and working facilities must be available which are suitable for the requirements of staff of both sexes. A place must be provided for the employees' outdoor clothing.

Staircases must be well lit and must have handrails. Equipment which is in any way dangerous must have its dangerous parts guarded. Employees must not be asked to lift loads which are liable to cause them injury.

First aid boxes must be available, and one member of staff must be in charge of and be competent in first aid. Other employees must not tamper with or interfere with these first aid materials.

The environmental health officers have right of entry and inspection at their convenience.

◆ Food Hygiene Regulations

Many of the points covered under the Offices, Shops and Railway Premises Act are also dealt with under the Food Hygiene (General) Regulations 1970 and the Food Hygiene (Scotland) Regulations 1959 as amended.

Beverages are regarded as food under these regulations, so beverages sales and service activities are governed by them.

Food and beverage business premises must be sanitary, and all equipment which is likely to come into contact with food and drink must be able to be kept clean and free from contamination. This equipment must then be kept clean.

The work area must be kept clear of accumulated refuse.

Food must be kept at least 450 mm (18 in) from the ground, but this does not include items such as sealed bottles.

All food rooms must be kept in a good state of repair and must be properly lit and ventilated.

Clean toilet facilities must be provided away from food areas and wash basins, water, soap, nail-brushes and hand drying facilities must also be provided. Notices must be displayed in the toilet areas telling employees to wash their hands after using the toilet.

All food and beverage sales and service staff must keep themselves and their clothes clean. All cuts and abrasions must be covered. Staff must not smoke, spit or take snuff in a food and beverage service area with open food. It is an offence under these regulations to smoke behind the bar. Employees suffering from certain diseases and illnesses must not work near food.

CHAPTER THREE

◆ *Restaurant personnel* ◆

SECTION ONE
Restaurant personnel involved in guéridon service

SECTION TWO
Job descriptions and specifications of restaurant personnel

Restaurant personnel involved in guéridon service

The size and the exclusiveness of an establishment is a determining factor in the structure of its restaurant brigade.

The waiting brigade is normally organized along traditional lines, which helps to determine their duties and responsibilities.

◆ Restaurant manager (directeur du restaurant)

The restaurant manager has the administrative and organizational responsibility for the food service areas. These would normally include restaurants, lounge, room service and ancillary areas. The standards of service are set by the manager.

The restaurant manager is involved in interviewing prospective new members of staff and is responsible for on- and off-the-job training. He or she will also be involved in the compiling of duty rotas and holiday lists.

Together with the head chef and the general manager, the restaurant manager plans menus and sets profit targets. He or she may also be involved in the planning of banquets.

◆ Head waiter (maître d'hôtel)

The head waiter has the overall responsibility for the day-to-day running of the restaurant. He or she is also responsible for ensuring that the correct standards of service are maintained. The head waiter will deal with customers' reservations and distribute the workload.

During the service, the head waiter will receive customers, escort them to their tables, and take their orders. Depending on the size and excellence of the operation, there may be more than one maître d'hôtel, in which case the duties and responsibilities are divided among them.

◆ Station head waiter (maître d'hôtel de carré)

The station head waiter has the responsibility for the service of a number of tables, usually five or six, seating about twenty customers, and is aided by a team of staff. The station head waiter will take the orders on his or her station (rang), particularly if customers walk directly into the restaurant without having an aperitif in the cocktail bar.

◆ Station waiter (chef de rang)

The station waiter is responsible for the standard of service on his or her station. Together with the station head waiter, the station waiter will prepare any dishes requiring special assembling or finishing.

◆ Demi-chef de rang

A demi-chef de rang is a waiter who is not as experienced as a station waiter. His or her duties will be of a similar nature, but the station will normally be smaller.

◆ Commis waiter (commis de rang or commis de suite)

A commis waiter is an apprentice waiter with limited experience. He or she will help the station waiter during service, and his or her main duties will include carrying food from the kitchen to the point of service, and distributing food checks to the kitken. A commis waiter is also responsible for keeping his or her sideboard stocked with equipment and, depending on experience, he or she may serve vegetables, sauces and accompaniments.

◆ Apprentice waiter (commis débarrasseur)

An apprentice waiter is a very junior member of the brigade whose main responsibilities are to ensure that all dirty items are removed to the wash up and to ensure that the sideboard is left clean and well stocked. He or she will be responsible for cleaning the restaurant during the *mise en place*. In establishments which do not employ appentice waiters, these duties would be carried out by the commis waiter.

It is important to bear in mind that job titles vary from one establishment to another. The majority of hotels and restaurants use the classical French titles but American companies use totally different names, for example, a station head waiter is known as a captain and a commis waiter has the unusual name of busboy.

It is also important to note that job specifications will also vary because the duties of restaurant staff are influenced by factors such as size and rating of establishment, choice and price range of menu offered, theme of restaurant and customer target.

◆ Wine waiter/waitress (sommelier)

The main responsibility of the wine waiter is the service of drinks. This includes all alcoholic and non-alcoholic beverages, cigars and cigarettes, but excludes after-dinner coffee.

The wine waiter should be able to advise customers, when required, on the choice of wines and be a good salesperson. Prior to the service commencing, he or she must ensure that the mise-en-place is ready. During the service the wine waiter will take orders for beverages from customers and serve them when required.

◆

The following are organizational charts showing how the classical restaurant brigade can be adapted to suit the different needs of individual establishments.

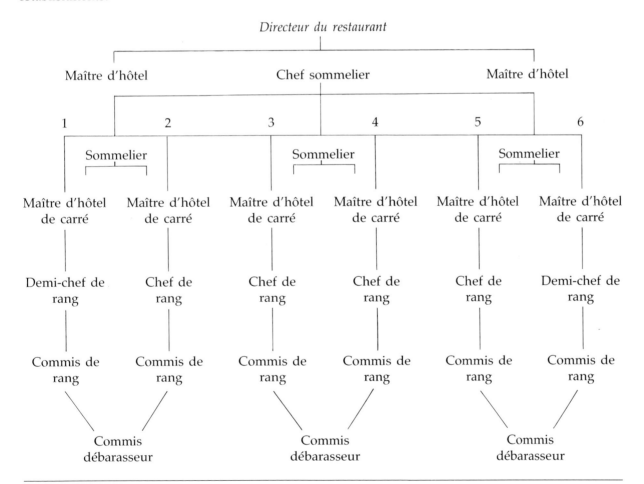

Figure 2 *An example of a chart which may be used in a 5-star hotel's restaurant to accommodate approximately 120 guests*

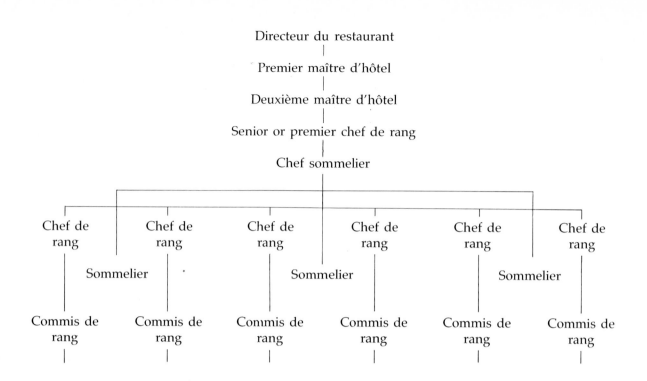

Figure 3 *This staffing structure shows a brigade where more responsibility is given to the chefs de rang, thus eliminating the maître d'hôtel de carré (station head waiter). The overall supervision of the restaurant is given to the senior chef de rang and two assistant restaurant managers. The restaurant would accommodate approximately 120 guests*

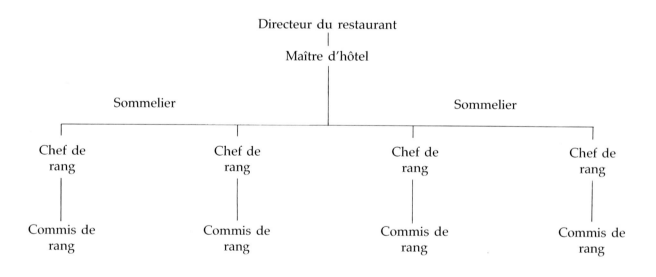

Figure 4 *This organizational chart may be used by a smaller establishment seating 60 to 80 customers. In this type of organization both the directeur du restaurant and the maître d'hôtel would be expected to take customers' orders and supervise the restaurant*

The following are examples of job descriptions and specifications.

◆ Restaurant manager/manageress

◆

Job description

Title:	Restaurant manager/manageress (Directeur du restaurant)
Department:	Food and beverage
Scope:	To profitably manage food and beverage service operations
Responsible to:	Food and beverage manager/manageress

Main responsibilities:

1 Organization and administration of Food and Beverage Service areas
2 Compilation of menus in conjunction with the head chef
3 Control of cash and liquid stock
4 Supervision of all food and beverage service personnel
5 Control of food and beverage service equipment
6 Duties rotas
7 Observance of Food Hygiene and Health and Safety Regulations
8 Staff training
9 Customer relationships
10 Setting and maintenance of standards
11 Achievement of profit and revenue targets
12 Assumption and acceptance of management responsibilities and tasks

---
◆

◆

Job specification

Job title:	Restaurant manager/ manageress (Directeur de restaurant)
Sex:	Male or female
Age:	Over 30
UK qualifications:	BTEC diploma in hotel and catering operations, CGLI master restaurateur, CGLI 707−1, 707−2

and 717

Desirable UK qualifications:	CGLI 706−1 and 706−2
Technical:	A good knowledge of and fluent in two languages
Experience:	Overall experience in all food and beverage service areas. Recent experience of controlling a similar establishment. Continental experience desirable
Qualities:	Ability to control staff, stable record of employment and trustworthy

Conditions of employment:
All meals supplied from the menu while on duty
Five days a week, 40 hours per week, split shifts
Five weeks' holiday per year plus recognized bank holidays

◆

◆ Head waiter/waitress

◆

Job description

Title:	Head waiter/waitress (Maître d'hôtel)
Department:	Food and beverage
Scope:	To assist the Restaurant manager in the running of all food and beverage service operations
Responsible to:	Restaurant manager/manageress

Main responsibilities:

1 Preparation and presentation of food and beverage service area
2 Supervision of service
3 Organization and coordination of staff activities
4 Motivation of staff
5 On-the-job training
6 Observance of Food Hygiene and Health and Safety Regulations
7 Customer relationship
8 Sales promotion
9 Taking of reservations and allocation of tables

◆

Job specification

Job title:	Head waiter/waitress (Maître d'hôtel)
Sex:	Male or female
Age:	Over 25
UK qualifications:	BTEC diploma in hotel and catering operations, CGLI master restaurateur, 707−1, 707−2 and 717
Desirable UK qualifications:	CGLI 706−2 and 706−1
Experience:	Overall experience in all food and beverage service areas. Recent experience of controlling a similar establishment. Continental experience desirable
Qualities:	Able to speak a language other than English − preferably French. Ability to organize and control staff. Stable record of employment. High level of social skills and trustworthy

Conditions of employment:
All meals supplied while on duty
Five days a week, 40 hours per week, split shifts
Five weeks' holiday per year

◆ Station head waiter/waitress

Job description

Title:	Station head waiter/waitress (Maître d'hôtel de carré)
Department:	Food and beverage
Scope:	To ensure that guests receive a high standard of service and hospitality

Responsible to: Restaurant manager/manageress
Main responsibilities:
1 To meet, greet and seat guests
2 To coordinate, supervise and maintain food and beverage service standards
3 Assist with the service

4 Control monies and billing
5 Ensure standards of hygiene and safety are met
6 Maintain high standards of customer relations
7 On-the-job training

Job specification

Job title:	Station head waiter/waitress (Maître d'hôtel de carré)
Sex:	Male or female
Age:	Over 23
UK qualifications:	CGLI 707−1, 707−2 and 717
Desirable UK qualifications:	CGLI 706−2 and 706−1
Experience:	Experience of running a station. Recent experience in a high-class establishment
Personal qualities:	Stable record of employment. Ability to organize. High level of social skills and trustworthy

Conditions of employment:
All meals supplied while on duty
Five days a week, 40 hours per week, split shifts
Five weeks' holiday per year

◆ Station waiter/waitress

Job description

Title:	Station waiter/waitress (Chef et demi-chef de rang)
Department:	Food and beverage
Scope:	To create the meal experience for all guests, by ensuring high standards of service, hospitality and social skills

Responsible to: Restaurant manager/manageress
Main responsibilities:
1 To meet, greet and seat guests
2 To provide a friendly and efficient service and ensure a high standard of hospitality on his/her station

3 To actively implement the agreed method of service
4 To implement selling techniques
5 To comply with Food Hygiene and Health and Safety Regulations
6 To maintain a high standard of personal appearance and hygiene
7 To present customer accounts and be responsible for all monies and revenue due
8 To accept any task as delegated by the management
9 Preparation of mise-en-place
10 To attend training sessions when required

———————————— ◆ ————————————

———————————— ◆ ————————————

Job specification

Job title:	Station waiter/ waitress (Chef et demi-chef de rang)
Sex:	Male or female
Age:	Over 20
UK qualifications:	CGLI 707−1, 707−2 and 717
Desirable UK qualifications:	706−1 and 706−2
Experience:	Experience in a variety of styles of service and establishments. Some continental experience desirable
Personal qualities:	Stable record of employment. Ability to discharge required duties. High level of social skills and trustworthy

Conditions of employment:
All meals provided while on duty
Five days a week, 40 hours per week, split shifts
Five weeks' holiday per year

———————————— ◆ ————————————

◆ Commis waiter/waitress

———————————— ◆ ————————————

Job description

Title:	Commis waiter/waitress (Commis de rang)
Department:	Food and beverage
Scope:	To assist with the provision of the

meal experience for all guests and to assume responsibilities as delegated by the station waiter/waitress

Responsible to: Restaurant manager/manageress
Main responsibilities:
1 To help in the provision of a friendly but efficient service and ensure a high standard of hospitality on his/her station
2 To comply with Food Hygiene and Health and Safety Regulations
3 To maintain a high standard of personal appearance and hygiene
4 To act according to the instruction given by the station waiter/waitress
5 To help with the preparation of the restaurant
6 The mise-en-place on his/her station
7 To accept any task as delegated by the management
8 To attend training sessions when required

———————————— ◆ ————————————

———————————— ◆ ————————————

Job specification

Job title:	Commis waiter/waitress (Commis de rang et commis débarasseur)
Sex:	Male or female
Age:	Over 17
UK qualifications:	CGLI 707−1, 707−2 desirable. Training in the form of day release to obtain qualifications is available
Experience:	Some experience in silver service
Personal qualities:	Ability to discharge required duties. High level of social skills and trustworthy

Conditions of employment:
All meals provided while on duty
Five day a week, 40 hours per week, split shifts
Five weeks' holiday per year

———————————— ◆ ————————————

◆ Wine waiter/waitress

———————————— ◆ ————————————

Job description

Title:	Wine waiter/waitress (Sommelier)
Department:	Food and beverage
Scope:	To ensure the efficient service of all alcoholic and non-alcoholic beverages and tobacco

Responsible to: Restaurant manager/manageress
Main responsibilities:

1 Prior to service, to ensure that all mise-en-place is ready
2 Meet and greet guests, present wine lists and take orders. Advise customers when required
3 Ensure that all drinks are correctly served and at the correct time
4 Keep tables clear of dirty glasses and remove them to the glass wash area
5 Comply with Food Hygiene and Health and Safety Regulations
6 Maintain a high standard of personal appearance and hygiene
7 Comply with the requirements of beverages control
8 To accept any task as delegated by the management
9 Attend training sessions when required

◆

Job specification

Job title:	Wine waiter/waitress (Sommelier)
Sex:	Male or female
Age:	Over 25
UK qualifications:	CGLI 707−1, 707−2 and 717 or WSET higher certificate
Experience:	In the service of food as well as beverages. Recent experience in a similar class establishment
Personal qualities:	Stable record of employment. Ability to organize. High level of social skills and trustworthy. Selling skills and techniques

Conditions of employment:
All meals provided while on duty
Five days a week, 40 hours per week, split shifts
Five weeks' holiday per year

◆

CHAPTER FOUR

◆ *Special equipment* ◆

In order to successfully carry out guéridon service and lamp work certain items of equipment are essential. Equipment requirements will vary depending on the extent of the menu offered, the guéridon service provided and flambé work carried out.

Selecting the right equipment for different types of establishment is very important. Prices can vary dramatically from one manufacturer to another, as can quality. To buy the cheapest equipment does not always make economic sense since replacing it can be quite expensive. In addition, inefficient equipment can be quite frustrating to staff and can, in turn, affect the standard of service.

When buying equipment it would be wise to ensure that:

- ◆ The equipment has a warranty.
- ◆ It is safe to operate.
- ◆ It is easy to operate.
- ◆ If possible, it can be put to several uses.
- ◆ It can be easily repaired.
- ◆ It can be easily replaced.

◆ Guéridons

Guéridons can vary from simple sidetables to purpose-built trolleys. They should be cleaned and polished frequently. Any wheels should be kept well-lubricated.

Some of the more modern trolleys have movable flaps which, when lifted in position, extend the working surface.

Ideally, the guéridon should be table high so that it fits comfortably against a customer's table and

therefore enables the guest to see the work being carried out.

◆ Flambé trolleys

Flambé trolleys have been developed specifically for the purpose of cooking at the table. Most of the trolleys are gas-fuelled, with one or two burners. The gas bottle is housed in a compartment under the burner.

Figure 5   *A gas-fuelled flambé trolley*

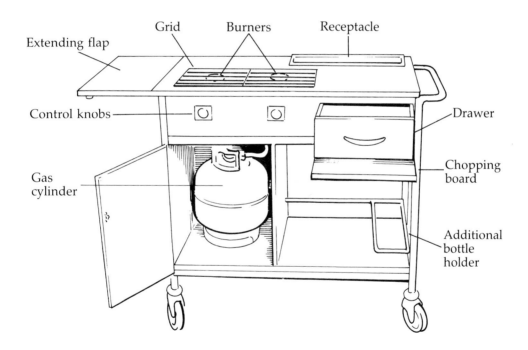

A different type of flambé trolley is one which is designed to take a flare lamp fuelled either by methylated spirits or gas.

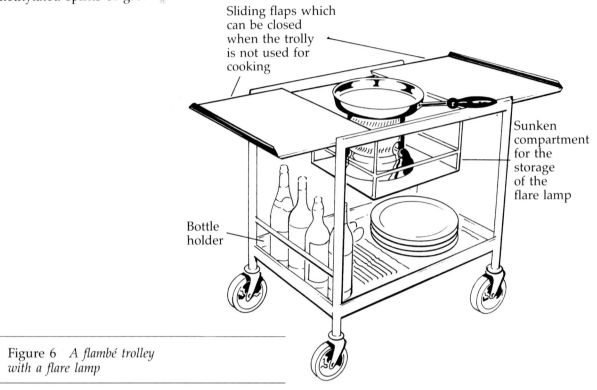

Sliding flaps which can be closed when the trolly is not used for cooking

Sunken compartment for the storage of the flare lamp

Bottle holder

Figure 6   *A flambé trolley with a flare lamp*

◆ Hot carving trolleys

There are several types of carving trolley on the market. They are a very expensive item to buy, but they are an excellent selling aid. The more traditional trolleys are silver-plated. However, the more recent models are made of stainless steel.

Carving trolleys can be heated by electricity or by methylated spirits.

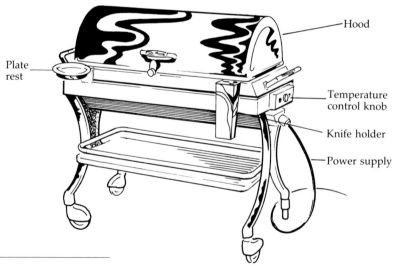

Plate rest

Hood

Temperature control knob

Knife holder

Power supply

Figure 7   *A hot carving trolley*

The food is placed on a carving board below which is a bain-marie containing hot water. The top of the bain-marie is covered with a hinged lid. The best type of trolley allows the waiter to open the lid towards himself, thus avoiding scalding. All bains-marie are provided with a safety steam outlet which should not be obstructed.

The trolley should be cleaned and the bain-marie should be drained at the end of each service. All movable parts should be washed in hot soapy water, dried and replaced.

Silver-plated trolleys should be regularly cleaned with plate powder, and they should be well-polished to ensure that the chemical does not taint the food. A small brush can be used to clean any elaborate design work.

◆ Hors d'oeuvre trolleys

There are several types of hors d'oeuvre trolley on the market. The most common type is the revolving trolley. Another type is the two-tier trolley.

The trolleys are usually made of stainless steel with raviers (small dishes) holding the food. A clean spoon should be used for each individual item of hors d'oeuvre.

After each service, the trolleys should be cleaned with hot soapy water.

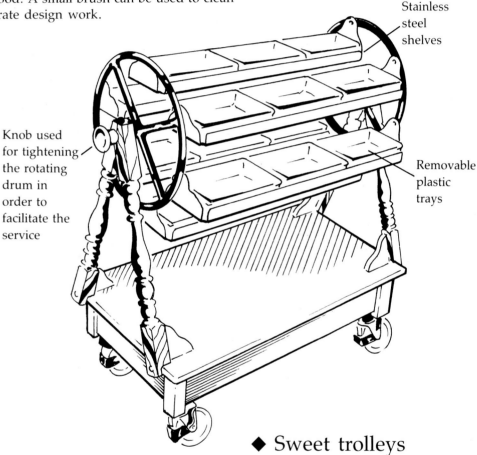

Knob used for tightening the rotating drum in order to facilitate the service

Stainless steel shelves

Removable plastic trays

Figure 8 *A hors d'oeuvre trolley*

◆ Sweet trolleys

Sweet trolleys are used to display all varieties of cold sweets served at the table. They consist of a stainless steel frame with two or three shelves, depending on the range of sweets offered.

Each sweet item should have its own separate utensils for service and they should be stocked with the sweet plates.

At the end of each service the trolleys should be thoroughly cleaned.

◆ *Lamps* ◆

There are several flare lamp designs on the market. However, there are only two acceptable fuels used for the purpose of cooking at the table. They are:

1 Butane gas.
2 Methylated spirits.

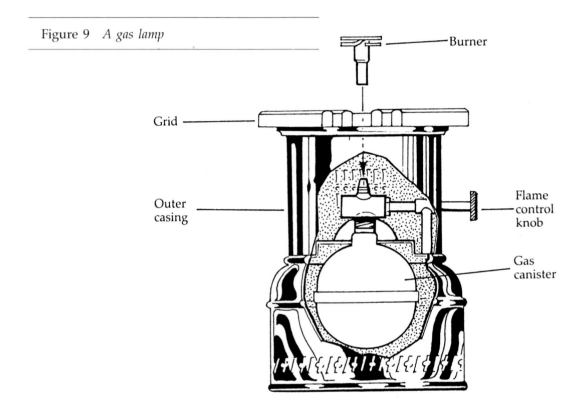

Figure 9 *A gas lamp*

◆ Care and maintenance of gas lamps

The lamp should be dismantled and all working parts cleaned. The gas jet should be cleared by blowing through it. No sharp objects should be used for this purpose as this could damage the burner and cause an uneven flame.

The outer casing of the lamp should be polished using the appropriate polishing agent.

The gas bottle should be checked and replaced if necessary. When replacing a gas bottle it should be carried out away from naked flames. The bottle should be tightened thoroughly and checked for leaks. The lamp should then be reassembled and checked to ensure that it is in working order.

◆ Care and maintenance of methylated spirits lamps

The lamp should be dismantled and all working parts cleaned. The wick should be trimmed and checked for length.

The reservoir should be filled with methylated spirits. This operation must be carried out away from naked flames.

The outer casing of the lamp should be polished with the appropriate cleaning agent.

Care should be taken that the lamp is not overfilled, that the burner is tightly secured and that any spillage of methylated spirits is wiped off.

Finally, the lamp should be reassembled and checked to ensure that it is in working order.

Figure 10   *Two types of methylated spirits lamp*

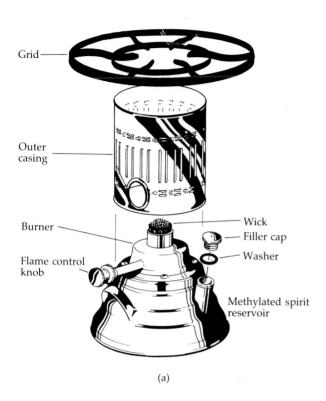

Grid

Outer casing

Burner

Flame control knob

Wick

Filler cap

Washer

Methylated spirit reservoir

(a)

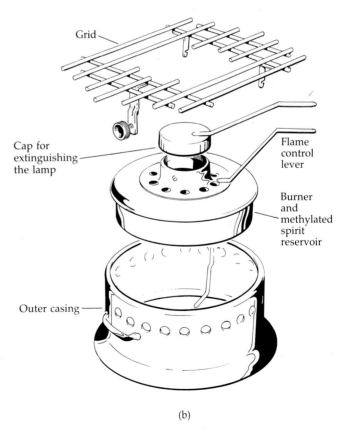

Grid

Cap for extinguishing the lamp

Flame control lever

Burner and methylated spirit reservoir

Outer casing

(b)

◆ *Suzette pans* ◆

The most suitable type of suzette pan is made from copper and is silver lined (to prevent the food from coming in to contact with the copper). It is safe to use an unlined copper pan to cook in, but food should not be allowed to cool down in the same container or copper poisoning could result.

Copper is the best material to use because it is a good conductor of heat, which is essential for cooking at table in the restaurant. These dishes require only a short cooking time and so if other types of metal pan are used, only the centre of the pan would become hot, thus making cooking very difficult.

The pan should be cleaned with copper cleaner on the outside and silver cleaner on the inside and then it should be washed thoroughly to remove any traces of polish.

Great care should be taken not to damage the silver lining of the pan.

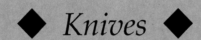

◆ *Knives* ◆

There is a very wide range of knives available. However, certain knives lend themselves to do some tasks better than others. From our experience, the following knives should be available for use in the restaurant:

◆ 100 mm (4 in) stainless steel paring knife.
   Usage: Preparation of fresh fruit.
◆ 150 mm (6 in) stainless steel knife.
   Usage: Preparation of large fruit, carving of poultry and small joints, for example, double entrecôte steak.
◆ 250 mm (10 in) stainless steel Granton knife.
   Usage: Slicing of York ham.
◆ 300 mm (12 in) stainless steel thin bladed knife.

Usage: Slicing of smoked salmon and Parma ham.
◆ 300 mm (12 in) stainless steel rigid blade knife.
   Usage: Slicing of large joint, for example, roast boned-sirloin of beef, roast leg of lamb, etc.

Traditionally, waiters used a specially sharpened table knife to carve in the restaurant. In our experience, this is no longer the case since the majority of establishments are now providing waiters with the correct and a wide range of equipment.

CHAPTER FIVE

Accompaniments ◆ *and covers* ◆ *for special dishes*

SECTION ONE
Hors d'oeuvres

SECTION TWO
Fish

SECTION THREE
Meat

NAME OF DISH			
◆ *French* ◆	*English* ◆	◆ *Description* ◆	
Cocktail de Florida	Florida cocktail	Segments of fresh orange and grapefruit served in a glass or silver coupe and decorated with a cherry.	
Melon charentais ou ogen	Charentais or ogen melon	Charentais: small round melons originating from France with orange-pink flesh. Ogen: small round melon from Israel with green flesh.	
Poire d'avocat	Avocado pear	Thick skinned, dark green fruit with a bland flavoured waxen textured flesh from Israel or South Africa.	
Poire d'avocat aux crevettes	Avocado pear with shrimps	Avocado pears filled with shrimps and laced with a Marie Rose sauce.	
Cocktail de crevettes	Shrimps cocktail	A cocktail made from shrimps laced with a Marie Rose sauce on a chiffonade of lettuce.	
Artichaut chaud au beurre fondu ou à l'hollandaise	Hot artichoke with melted butter or hollandaise sauce	The flower of the artichoke plant. Pale green in colour. The thick part of the leaves should be eaten first followed by the bottom.	
Huitres	Oysters	Shellfish which can be eaten raw or cooked. Served by the dozen or half-dozen. The best English oysters are from Whitstable or Colchester. Oysters should be served fresh and cold.	
Artichaut froid à la vinaigrette	Cold artichoke with vinaigrette sauce		
Saumon fumé	Smoked salmon	The best salmon comes from Scotland. However, an excellent quality salmon is produced on the River Rhine in Germany. A side of salmon can weigh 2–2.5 kg (4–5 lb).	
Truite fumée	Smoked trout	Most smoked trout comes from trout farms.	
Asperges chauds au beurre fondu ou à l'hollandaise	Hot asparagus with melted butter or hollandaise sauce	A green or white stick-like vegetable. Best varieties are Argenteuil or Evesham. Should be served from an asparagus rack. Can be served as an hors d'oeuvres substitute or as a separate vegetable course.	
Asperges froids à la vinaigrette ou à la mayonnaise	Cold asparagus with vinaigrette sauce or mayonnaise		

◆ Cover ◆	◆ Accompaniment ◆	◆ Season ◆
200 mm (8 in) underplate, doiley and teaspoon.	Castor sugar.	All year.
200 mm (8 in) underplate in a glass or silver coupe on crushed ice.	Castor sugar and ginger or port wine.	Charentaise: June to October. Ogen: March to November.
200 mm (8 in) underplate, doiley, avocado dish and teaspoon.	Vinaigrette sauce.	All year.
200 mm (8 in) underplate, doiley, avocado pear dish, teaspoon and fish fork.	Brown bread and butter, cayenne pepper and pepper mill.	All year.
200 mm (8 in) underplate, doiley, glass or silver coupe, teaspoon and fish plate.	Brown bread and butter, cayenne pepper and pepper mill.	All year.
Artichoke plate, joint fork and fingerbowl.	Melted butter or hollandaise sauce.	August to October.
Oyster plate and oyster fork and finger bowl. If an oyster plate an oyster plate is not available a welled soup plate filled with crushed ice can be used.	Cayenne pepper, pepper mill tabasco, chilli, vinegar, lemon wedge, brown bread and butter.	September to April.
Artichoke plate, joint fork and fingerbowl.	Sauce vinaigrette.	August to October.
Fish plate, fish knife and fork.	Brown bread and butter, cayenne pepper and peppermill, and lemon.	All year.
Cold fish plate, fish knife and fork.	Brown bread and butter, cayenne pepper and peppermill, lemon and horseradish sauce.	All year.
Hot joint plate, fingerbowl and asparagus tongs if required.	Melted butter or hollandaise sauce.	May to June/July.
Cold joint plate, finger-bowl and asparagus tongs if required.	Vinaigrette sauce or mayonnaise.	May to June/July.

NAME OF DISH			◆ Description ◆
◆ French ◆	English	◆	
Épis de maïs	Corn on the cob		Can be served as an hors d'oeuvres substitute or as a separate vegetable course.
Pâté de foie gras	Goose liver pâté		The first recorded pâté de foie gras was made in 1782 by Monsieur Clause on commission from the Military Commander of Alsace. A few years later he opened a shop in Strasbourg where he sold his pâtés. This city has since become renowned for the production of the famous dish. The geese are fed on a rich diet which causes the liver to swell. This is the part used for the pâté. A black truffle is added during the packaging.
Jambon de Parme	Parma ham		There are several varieties of cured hams, the best hams are made in Parma. They are produced by rubbing a mixture of salt and saltpetre on the hams and allowing them to hang for several months to mature.
Caviar	Caviar		This is the carefully salted roe of the fish of the sturgeon family. The main supply and highest quality caviar comes from Russia from the Port of Astrakhan, where the River Volga flows into the Caspian Sea. The best-known types are the *beluga*, a fish of large proportions bearing more than three hundred pounds of finest caviar; the *ocietrova* or sturgeon; and the *sevruga*, which is of a higher quality than the first two caviars.

◆ Cover ◆	◆ Accompaniment ◆	◆ Season ◆
200 mm (8 in) plate, doiley, corn on the cob dish and holders.	Melted butter.	July to September.
Small knife and cold fish plate.	Hot finger toast and butter.	
Small knife and fork and cold fish plate.	Melon or fresh figs when they are in season.	
Caviar knife and cold fish plate.	Hot finger toast and unsalted butter or Blinis (Buckwheat pancakes). A popular way of serving caviar is to accompany it with lemon, sieved hardboiled egg white and chopped shallots.	All year.

NAME OF DISH		
French ◆	*English* ◆	◆ *Description* ◆
Truite au bleu	Blue trout	In order to achieve the blue coloration of the skin, the trout must be cooked immediately after it is killed. The change in colour is caused by the reaction of the vinegar in the court-bouillon on the slime of fish. The skin should be removed before serving the trout to the customer. The trout should be served in a trout kettle.
Truite meunière	Pan-fried trout	The best trout are those caught in the wild. The rainbow trout is not native to this country and is mostly the product of trout farms. The only indigenous trout is the brown trout which is found in abundance in the Scottish rivers and lochs.
Darne de saumon grillée	Grilled cut of salmon on the bone	Scottish salmon is reputed to be the best. However, some of the English rivers can produced good quality fish. Today, farmed salmon is big business and enables the caterer to offer salmon throughout the year.
Darne de saumon pochée chaude	Hot poached cut of salmon on the bone	
Saumon froid	Cold salmon	
Tronçon de turbot poché	Hot poached turbot on the bone	One of the best flat fish with a beautiful delicate flavour. The flesh is firm and white.
Tronçon de turbot grillé	Hot grilled turbot on the bone	
Sole de Douvre grillée	Grilled Dover sole	One of the best white fish. Has a firm delicate flavour and lends itself to a variety of cooking.
Sole de Douvre frite	Fried Dover sole	
Homard froid	Cold lobster	Found in all European seas. Overfishing has resulted in a reduction of catchments making this dish expensive. However, extensive lobster farming in Scotland should help to alleviate the situation. A lobster takes a long time to grow. A fully grown lobster will weigh from 1 kg (2 lb) upwards and will be at least 10 years old.

◆ Cover ◆	◆ Accompaniment ◆	◆ Season ◆
Fish knife and fork, and hot fish plate.	Melted butter (beurre fondu) or hollandaise sauce.	March to October depending on the river, although available all year from trout farms.
Fish knife and fork, and hot fish plate.		March to October.
Fish knife and fork, and hot fish plate.	Béarnaise sauce.	February to September, although available all year round from salmon farms.
Fish knife and fork, and hot fish plate.	Hollandaise sauce.	February to September.
Fish knife and fork, and cold fish plate.	Mayonnaise and cucumber salad.	February to September.
Fish knife and fork, and hot fish plate.	Beurre fondu or hollandaise sauce.	February to September.
Fish knife and fork, and hot fish plate.	Béarnaise sauce.	February to September.
Fish knife and fork, and hot fish plate.	Beurre maître d'hôtel, tartare, remoulade or bearnaise sauces.	All year, but sole in the spring is of poor quality.
Fish knife and fork, and hot fish plate.	Tartare sauce or remoulade sauce.	
Fish knife and fork, cold fish plate, lobster pick and finger bowl.	Mayonnaise.	All year but best in summer.

NAME OF DISH			
◆ *French* ◆	*English* ◆	◆ *Description* ◆	
Entrecôte double	Double sirloin steak	A boneless cut of sirloin weighing about 500 g (1 lb). Served to two covers.	
Châteaubriand	Double fillet steak	A cut from the thick part of the fillet steak weighing about 500 g (1 lb). Served to a minimum of two covers.	
Selle d'agneau rôtie ou Poelée	Saddle of lamb roasted or pot roasted	A cut of lamb on the bone comprising the two loins, the chumps and the tail (long saddle) or two loins (short saddle).	
Carré d'agneau rôti ou poelée	Best end of lamb roasted or pot roasted	A cut of lamb on the bone comprising about six cutlets.	
Râble de lievre rôtie	Roast saddle of hare	The hare should be hung upside down for a week in a refrigerator before use. The saddle is usually marinated before cooking.	
Poulet rôti a l'Anglaise	Roast chicken English style	Whole roast chicken. After carving, a piece of dark and white meat should be served to each customer.	
Caneton rôti a l'Anglaise	Roast duckling English style	Whole roasted duckling. Normally only the breast is served.	
Grouse rôtie à l'Anglaise	Roast grouse English style	A game bird found in the Highlands of Scotland. It should be served cut in half.	
Faisan rôti à l'Anglaise	Roast pheasant English style	One of the best known game birds.	
Canard sauvage à la presse	Pressed wild duck	This dish is not often served in this country, but on the Continent it can still be found in top-class establishments. It requires lengthy preparation at the guéridon using special equipment. The first part of the operation is to remove the legs and the skin. Carve the breast as for roast wild duck. Next the carcass is placed into the press and squeezed tightly to extract the juices. The juices are then used to produce the sauce which will finish the dish.	
Canard sauvage rôti	Roast wild duck	The duck should be hung at least 24 hours before cooking and should not be overcooked as it becomes dry and tough. After presentation to the customer, the legs are removed (but not served). The breast is then carved in thin slices called aiguillettes. The legs can be used to make game pâtés, salmis or bortsch.	
Steak tartare	Steak tartare	A finely chopped fillet steak prepared at the guéridon. It originates from Eastern Europe and is eaten raw.	

◆ Cover ◆	◆ Accompaniment ◆	◆ Season ◆
Steak knife, joint fork and hot joint plate.	Béarnaise sauce and French or English mustard.	All year.
Steak knife, joint fork and hot joint plate.	Béarnaise sauce and French or English mustard.	All year.
Joint knife and fork, and hot joint plate.	Roast gravy and mint sauce or redcurrant jelly.	All year, but best in the summer.
Joint knife and fork, and hot joint plate.	Roast gravy and mint sauce or redcurrant jelly.	All year.
Joint knife and fork, and hot joint plate.	Roast gravy and redcurrant jelly.	August to February.
Joint knife and fork, and hot joint plate.	Roast gravy, stuffing and bread sauce.	All year.
Joint knife and fork, and hot joint plate.	Roast gravy, stuffing and apple sauce.	All year.
Joint knife and fork, and hot joint plate.	Roast gravy, fried breadcrumbs and bread sauce.	12 August to 12 December.
Joint knife and fork, and hot joint plate.	Roast gravy, bread sauce and fried breadcrumbs.	1 October to 11 February.
Joint knife and fork, and hot joint plate.		August to March.
Joint knife and fork, and hot joint plate.	Orange salad with acidulated cream dressing, roast gravy and fried breadcrumbs.	August to March.
Joint knife and fork, and joint plate.	Hot toast and butter.	All year.

CHAPTER SIX

◆ *Technical skills* ◆

SECTION ONE
The preparation of hors d'oeuvres

SECTION TWO
The preparation of fish

SECTION THREE
The preparation of flambé dishes

SECTION FOUR
Part I: Carving techniques
Part II: Dishes requiring special attention

SECTION FIVE
The preparation of fresh fruit

SECTION SIX
The preparation of speciality coffees

SECTION SEVEN
Glossary

Cocktail de Florida
Florida Cocktail

Two covers

◆ Ingredients

2 grapefruits
2 oranges
2 maraschino cherries
Castor sugar

◆ Equipment

1 joint plate to peel the fruits
2 sweet plates for the segments
2 service spoons and forks
1 × 100 mm (4 in) sharp paring knife
2 glass coupes on underplates with doileys
1 clean serviette

2. Using a service spoon and fork, transfer the grapefruit on to a clean plate.

3. Hold the grapefruit steady with the fork and cut the end of the fruit which has been attached to the tree.

4. Turn the fruit cut-side down and push the fork through the cut end and into the centre of the grapefruit.

5. Make an incision round the grapefruit at the opposite end taking care not to cut through the flesh.

6. Peel the grapefruit from the cut end toward the fork. Cut the skin in thin strips and remove any white pith.

7. Separate the segments on to a clean 200 mm (8 in) plate by cutting between the membranes.

8

Note the separate membranes.

9

Repeat the above operation with a fresh orange.

10

The finished segments and peelings.

11

Arrange alternate segments into a glass coupe.

12

Decorate with a cherry and place on a doilyed 200 mm (8 in) plate with a teaspoon. Serve separately a little caster sugar.

Melon Charentais ou Ogen
Charentais or Ogen Melon

Two covers

1

◆ Equipment

1 joint plate to cut the melon on
1 soup plate for the seed
2 silver coupes on underplates
  with doileys
1 clean serviette
1 × 150 mm (6 in) stainless steel
  knife
1 service spoon and fork
1 dessert spoon

◆ Ingredients

1 medium-sized charentais melon
2 measures of tawny port
Castor sugar
Crushed ice

2

Transfer the melon on to the clean joint plate using a service spoon and fork.

3

Hold the melon steady with a clean serviette and cut evenly in half.

4

Holding the melon half in the serviette, scoop out the seeds into a soup plate using a dessert spoon.

5

Score the melon with a spoon and place into a dish of crushed ice.

6

Fill the well in the centre with port and serve on a doileyed 200 mm (8 in) plate. Serve separately a little castor sugar.

Poire d'Avocat aux Crevettes
Avocado Pear with Shrimps

Two covers

1

Note: Cut the avocado pear as demonstrated on pages 52 and 53.
Prepare sauce Marie Rose as demonstrated on page 54.

◆ Ingredients

1 ripe avocado pear
50 g (2 oz) peeled shrimps
45 ml ($1\frac{3}{4}$ fl oz) mayonnaise
25 ml (1 fl oz) cream
Tomato ketchup
Worcester sauce
Lemon juice
Salt
Cayenne pepper
$\frac{1}{4}$ lemon
$\frac{1}{4}$ measure brandy

◆ Equipment

1 soup plate for the sauce
2 sweet plates for the debris and for the cutlery
2 service spoons and forks
1 sharp paring knife
2 avocado dishes on underplates with doileys
1 clean serviette
1 teaspoon

2

Hold the avocado pear with a clean serviette and scoop out two thirds of the flesh with a teaspoon.

3

Place the flesh into the prepared Marie Rose sauce.

4

Add the shrimps and blend.

5

Fill the cavity of the avocado pear with the mixture.

6

Dust with cayenne pepper.

7

The finished dish with accompaniments.

◆ *Poire d'Avocat à la Vinaigrette* ◆
Avocado Pear Vinaigrette

Two covers

1

◆ *Ingredients*

1 ripe avocado pear	Salt
3 tablespoons olive oil	Pepper
1 tablespoon wine vinegar	French mustard

◆ *Equipment*

1 soup plate for the vinaigrette
1 sweet plate for the debris
1 service spoon and fork
1 × 100 mm (4 in) sharp paring knife
1 clean serviette
2 avocado dishes on underplates with doileys
1 teaspoon

2

Make the vinaigrette sauce. Place salt, pepper and French mustard into the soup plate.

3

Add one tablespoon of wine vinegar.

4

Blend the seasoning and vinegar using a service fork.

5

Add three tablespoons of olive oil.

6

Blend thoroughly.

7

Transfer the avocado pear to a clean serviette.

8

Using a sharp 100 mm (4 in) paring knife, cut the avocado pear in half lengthways.

9

Grip the two halves and twist in opposite directions. Place the half without the stone on to an 200 mm (8 in) plate.

10

Tap the stone sharply with the heel of the paring knife.

11

Twist the knife and remove the stone.

12

Score the flesh of the pear.

13

Place the prepared halves into avocado dishes and fill the cavities with the vinaigrette sauce. Serve on a doileyed 200 mm (8 in) plate with a teaspoon.

14

The finished dish.

◆ *Cocktail de Crevettes à la Sauce Marie Rose* ◆
Shrimp Cocktail with Marie Rose Sauce

One cover

◆ Ingredients

50 g (2 oz) peeled shrimps
10 g ($\frac{1}{3}$ oz) chiffonade of lettuce
45 ml ($1\frac{3}{4}$ fl oz) mayonnaise
25 ml (1 fl oz) double cream
Tomato ketchup
Lemon juice
Worcester sauce
Salt
$\frac{1}{4}$ Lemon
Cayenne pepper
$\frac{1}{4}$ measure brandy
1 slice brown bread
Butter

◆ Equipment

1 soup plate for the sauce
1 sweet plate for the cutlery
2 service spoons and forks
1 glass coupe on an underplate
  with a doiley
1 clean serviette
1 teaspoon
1 fish fork

2

Scoop the mayonnaise into a soup plate.

3

Add a few dashes of Worcester sauce.

4

Add the Brandy.

5

Add the double cream.

6

Add the lemon juice and blend using a service spoon.

7

Add the tomato ketchup until a light pink colour is achieved.

8

Add the seasoned shrimps and toss in the sauce until coated.

9

Place the chiffonade of lettuce into the bottom of the coupes.

10

Carefully cover the chiffonade with the prepared shrimps.

11

Dust with cayenne pepper.

12

Serve on a 200 mm (8 in) doileyed plate with a teaspoon, fish fork, lemon wedge and brown bread and butter.

Truite Fumée ◆
Smoked Trout

Two covers

◆ *Ingredients*

2 smoked trout
½ lemon
Lettuce

◆ *Equipment*

1 × 100 mm (4 in) stainless steel paring knife
1 service spoon and fork
1 joint plate to skin the trout on
3 cold fish plates
1 spare serviette

Transfer the smoked trout on to a cold joint plate.

Remove the head using a sharp 100 mm (4 in) knife.

Remove the tail.

Method 1

Cut lengthways along the belly of the fish.

Slide the service spoon between the skin and the flesh.

7

Push the skin back.

8

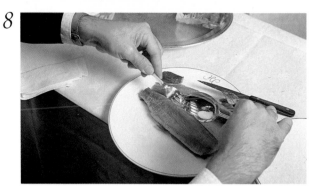

Roll the trout clean of the skin.

Method 2

9

Cut lengthways along the belly and the back of the fish.

10

Pierce the skin at the head with the service fork and roll the skin back on the fork.

11

Turn the trout and repeat the operation.

12

Serve on a bed of lettuce with lemon.

One cover

1

◆ *Ingredients*

1 hot globe artichoke
25 ml (1 fl oz) melted butter

◆ *Equipment*

1 artichoke plate
1 service spoon and fork
1 sauce ladle
1 spare serviette
1 finger bowl

2

Remove the choke from the artichoke.

3

Place on an artichoke plate and fill the centre with melted butter.

One cover

1

6–12 oysters, depending on their size
½ lemon

◆ *Equipment*

1 oyster plate or soup plate on underplate
1 service spoon and fork
1 clean serviette

2

Transfer the lemon to the centre of the oyster plate.

3

Place the oysters into the wells of the plate with their pointed ends facing into the centre.

4

The completed dish. (Note the dish of crushed ice.)

5

An alternative method of serving oysters using a welled soup plate filled with crushed ice.

◆ *Saumon Fumé* ◆
Smoked Salmon

One cover

1

Note: The salmon should have been prepared ready for carving beforehand.

◆ *Ingredients*

1 prepared smoked salmon on its board
$\frac{1}{4}$ lemon

◆ *Equipment*

1 pair fish tweezers
1 service spoon and fork
1 × 300 mm (12 in) stainless steel granton knife
2 fish plates
1 clean serviette

2

Before carving extract the long bones embedded in the flesh using a pair of tweezers.

3

Carve wafer thin slices of salmon, working from head to tail. *Note*: the first slice should be discarded as it is too strongly flavoured.

4

Continue carving and arrange the slices neatly on a cold 200 mm (8 in) plate.

5

Remove the dark flesh by cutting a 'V' incision. This should not be served as it contains bitter oils.

6

The finished dish.

Asperges Chauds au Beurre Fondu
Hot Asparagus with Melted Butter

One cover

◆ Ingredients

6–9 asparagus sticks, depending on the thickness of their sticks

25 ml (1 fl oz) melted butter

◆ Equipment

1 service spoon and fork
1 joint fork
1 hot joint plate
1 sauce ladle
1 spare serviette
1 pair asparagus tongs
1 fingerbowl

Transfer the asparagus on to a hot joint plate.

Place a joint fork under the joint plate in order to tilt it from right to left (this should be done at the table). Coat only the tips of the asparagus with melted butter.

Serve with a fingerbowl and asparagus tongs.

Épis de Maïs au Beurre Fondu
Corn on the Cob with Melted Butter

Two covers

◆ Ingredients

2 corn on the cobs
45 ml (1¾ fl oz) melted butter

◆ Equipment

2 pairs of corn on the cob holders
2 hot sweet plates
1 sauce ladle

Transfer the corn on the cob to a hot 200 mm (8 in) plate.

Insert the holders at either end of the corn.

Baste with melted butter.

The finished item ready for service.

Pâté de Foie Gras en Terrine
Goose Liver Pâté

One cover

◆ *Ingredients*

1 × 75 g (2$\frac{1}{2}$ oz) terrine of goose pâté on ice

◆ *Equipment*

1 sharp paring knife
2 teaspoons
1 jug of hot water
1 spare joint plate
1 cold fish plate
1 clean serviette

1

Note: Always check that the seal of the terrine is unbroken before removing the lid. Here the lid has been removed.

2

Transfer the pâté on to a plate. Take a teaspoon from the jug of hot water and wipe it with a clean serviette.

3

Draw the spoon across the surface of the pâté, allowing it to form a curl.

4

Place the curls on to a 200 mm (8 in) plate.

5

Serve six to eight curls per portion.

Jambon de Parme
Parma Ham

Two covers

◆ Ingredients

1 ham on its stand

◆ Equipment

1 service spoon and fork
1 × 300 mm (12 in) thin bladed knife
1 spare plate for the debris
2 cold fish plates
1 clean serviette

Trim excess fat from the front of the ham.

Trim excess fat from the back of the ham.

Hold the ham steady with a clean serviette and commence slicing wafer thin slices. Note the flap of fat retained to keep the ham fresh while not in use.

Lift each slice of ham with a fork.

Depending on the size of the ham, place three or four slices per person on a 200 mm (8 in) plate.

Replace the protective flap of fat over the ham to keep it fresh and moist. Note debris plate for trimmed fat.

Two covers

Note: Always check that the caviar seal is unbroken before removing the lid. Here the lid has been removed.

◆ Ingredients

1 100 g (3½ oz) jar of caviar on ice
Chopped shallots
Sieved hard boiled egg white and yolk (optional)
Chopped parsley
1 lemon, halved

◆ Equipment

5 teaspoons	1 spare plate for cutlery
2 cold fish plates	1 clean serviette

Delicately scoop out the caviar from the jar.

Use an additional teaspoon to ease the caviar on to the plate. Take care not to squash the eggs. Repeat the operation with the other plate.

Add the chopped shallots.

Add the chopped parsley.

Add the lemon.

Serve with either Blinis or hot finger toast and unsalted butter.

Truite au Bleu au Beurre Fondu
Blue Trout with Melted Butter

One cover

◆ Ingredients

1 × 225 g (8 oz) trout
25 ml (1 fl oz) melted butter

◆ Equipment

1 cold 200 mm (8 in) plate for the cutlery and the
  debris
1 hot joint plate
1 service spoon and fork
1 fish knife and fork
1 clean serviette

Transfer the cooked trout on to a hot joint plate.

Make an incision along the belly of the trout.

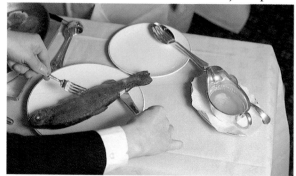

Turn the plate and make an incision along the
back of the trout.

Insert the fish knife delicately between the skin
and the flesh and peel the skin from the back to
the belly. Transfer the skin to the debris plate.
Turn the trout over and repeat the operation.

Serve the melted butter separately.

Trout ready for service.

Truite Meunière
Pan-Fried Trout

Two covers

◆ Ingredients

2 trout
50 g (2 oz) butter
Lemon juice
Parsley
Garnish

◆ Equipment

2 service spoons and forks
1 plate for the debris
2 hot fish plates
1 clean serviette

2 Remove head of trout and place on a debris plate.

3 Remove tail of trout and place on a debris plate. Note that the head and tail are broken off not cut off.

4 Remove the garnish to one side of the flat.

5 Transfer the trout on to a hot fish plate.

6 Remove the dorsal fin.

7 Sever any remaining skin along the belly of the trout.

8

Turn the trout on to its back and push down gently with the service spoon until the trout opens on to the plate.

9

Remove the backbone with a spoon and fork and place on debris plate.

10

Remove any remaining bones.

11

Replace the garnish and coat with brown butter and parsley (beurre noisette).

◆ *Tronçon de Turbot Poché a l'Hollandaise* ◆
Hot Poached Turbot with Hollandaise Sauce

One cover

◆ *Ingredients*

1 × 175 g (6 oz) tronçon of turbot
25 ml (1 fl oz) hollandaise sauce
Garnish

◆ *Equipment*

1 service spoon and fork
1 plate for the debris
2 hot joint plates

Transfer the tronçon on to a hot joint plate.

Remove the dark skin by rolling it on to the prongs of a service fork. Place it on a debris plate.

Repeat the operation with the other side.

Hold the tronçon steady with the fork and ease the flesh away from the bone using a service spoon.

Remove the wing bones and place on the debris plate.

Detach the backbone and place it on the debris plate.

8

Remove the white skin using a service spoon. Do not attempt to roll the skin as it is very soft and has a tendency to break.

9

Remove the remaining backbones.

10

Transfer the portioned turbot on to a clean, hot joint plate.

11

Decorate with garnish.

12

Serve with hollandaise sauce.

13

The finished dish.

Sole de Douvre Grillée
◆ Grilled Dover Sole

One cover

◆ Ingredients

1 Dover sole
Garnish

◆ Equipment

1 service spoon and fork
1 cold plate for the debris
1 hot fish plate
1 hot joint plate to fillet the sole

Remove the tail and place on a debris plate.

Remove the head and place on a debris plate.

Remove the garnish to one side of the flat.

Transfer the sole on to a hot joint plate.

Remove the side bones and place on to a debris plate.

Gently prise the two top fillets apart.

8

Run the spoon along the backbone from tail to head to loosen the bone from the flesh.

9

Insert the spoon under the bone and lift clean. Care should be taken not to lift any flesh with the bone.

10

Separate the two bottom fillets.

11

Reassemble on the flat.

12

Darne de Saumon Grillée à la Sauce Béarnaise
◆ ◆
Grilled Salmon with Béarnaise Sauce

One cover

◆ *Ingredients*

1 darne of salmon
25 ml (1 fl oz) béarnaise sauce

◆ *Equipment*

1 hot joint plate
1 service spoon and fork
1 plate for the debris
1 hot fish plate
1 clean serviette

1

2

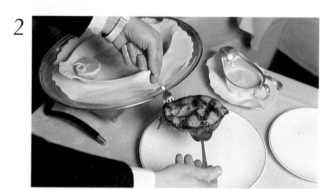

Transfer the salmon on to a hot joint plate.

3

Insert the prongs of the fork between the skin and the flesh and detach the skin.

4

Remove the skin by rolling the fork round the outside of the salmon.

5

Transfer the skin to the debris plate.

6

Insert the prongs of the fork into the centre of the backbone and gently pull the bone free.

7

Transfer to a clean, hot fish plate.

Sole de Douvre Frite
◆ Fried Dover Sole ◆

One cover

◆ *Ingredients*

1 sole

◆ *Equipment*

1 service spoon and fork
1 cold plate for the debris
1 hot fish plate
1 hot joint plate to fillet the sole

1

2

Remove the tail and transfer to the debris plate.

3

Remove the head and transfer to the debris plate.

4

Insert two joint forks through the fish on opposite sides of the backbone and prise both sets of fillets apart.

5

Continue down the whole length of the fish.

6

Remove the backbone and place on the debris plate.

Serve on a hot joint plate.

One cover

1

Cold lobster ready for service.

◆ *Ingredients*

1 × 1 kg (2 lb) cooked lobster, halved
½ lemon
Lettuce
Mayonnaise

Note: A larger lobster would normally be served for two covers.

◆ *Equipment*

1 lobster pick	1 clean serviette
1 service spoon and fork	1 fingerbowl
1 cold joint plate	

2

Pierce the tail end of the lobster with the service fork.

3

Hold the lobster steady with the spoon and pull the flesh free from the shell.

4

Place the lobster on to a clean joint plate together with the empty thorax.

5

Repeat the operation with the other half.

6

Transfer the cracked claw on to a clean serviette.

7

Remove the flesh from the claw using a lobster pick.

8

Place the flesh from the claw into the empty thorax.

9

Garnish with lemon and lettuce. Serve with mayonnaise.

Tortue Claire
◆ Clear Turtle Soup ◆

One cover

◆ Ingredients

1 portion turtle soup in a tureen
1 measure dry sherry

◆ Equipment

1 flare lamp
1 soup ladle
1 sauce ladle
1 hot consommé cup, saucer and underplate

Place the soup tureen on the lamp and remove the lid. Place the accompaniments on the table.

Lift the consommé cup to the tureen and ladle the hot soup into it, ensuring none is spilt into the saucer.

Pour a measure of dry sherry into a soup ladle.

Heat the sherry over the lamp and set it alight.

Pour the flaming sherry into the soup and serve.

Bisque de Homard ◆
◆ Lobster Bisque

One cover

◆ Ingredients

1 portion lobster bisque in a tureen
$\frac{1}{2}$ measure brandy
25 ml (1 fl oz) double cream

◆ Equipment

1 flare lamp
1 sauce ladle
1 soup ladle
1 hot consommé cup, saucer and underplate

Ladle the bisque into the consomme cup.

Pour a half measure of brandy into a small ladle.

Heat the brandy over a flare lamp and set it alight.

Pour the flaming brandy gently into the soup. It should float on top of the bisque.

Finish with double cream.

Scampi à la Newburg
Newburg Scampi

One cover

◆ Ingredients

150 g (6 oz) jumbo scampi
   rolled in flour
25 g (1 oz) butter
100 ml ($3\frac{1}{2}$ fl oz) lobster sauce
100 ml ($3\frac{1}{2}$ fl oz) double cream
1 measure dry sherry
1 measure brandy
Salt and cayenne pepper
1 portion hot pilaff rice (to be
   brought in from the kitchen
   when the dish is cooked)

◆ Equipment

1 flare lamp
1 suzette pan
2 service spoons and forks
2 cold joint plates for the
   cutlery and to rest the
   pan on
1 hot fish plate
1 clean serviette

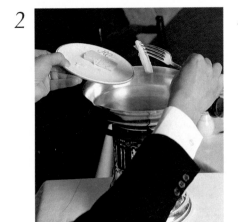

Place the butter into the
suzette pan.

When the butter is hot, add the
floured scampi. Seal the scampi
and sauté gently.

Season.

Deglaze the pan with a
measure of dry sherry.

Add a measure of brandy

Flame.

8

Add the lobster sauce

9

Add the double cream and blend together.

10

Using a clean spoon and fork, place the pilaff rice on a hot 200 mm (8 in) plate and make a well using the back of the service spoon.

11

Place the scampi and sauce into the well.

12

Dust the finished dish with cayenne pepper.

Scampi à la Provençale
Provençale Scampi

One cover

Ingredients

150 g (6 oz) jumbo scampi rolled in flour
25 g (1 oz) butter
12 ml olive oil
100 ml ($3\frac{1}{2}$ fl oz) cooked, chopped tomatoes with garlic
50 ml ($1\frac{3}{4}$ fl oz) dry white wine
1 measure brandy
Chopped parsley
Salt and pepper
1 portion hot pilaff rice (to be brought in from the kitchen when the dish is cooked)

◆ Equipment

1 flare lamp
1 suzette pan
2 service spoons and forks
2 cold joint plates for the cutlery and to rest the pan on
1 hot fish plate
1 clean serviette

Place the butter and oil in the suzette pan and heat until they are hot.

Season the floured scampi.

Add the scampi to the hot oil and butter and sauté quickly.

Deglaze the pan with the dry white wine.

6

Add the measure of brandy and flame.

7

Add the chopped tomatoes and blend with the scampi.

8

Place the scampi in the centre of a hot fish plate.

9

Using a clean spoon, surround the scampi with the pilaff rice.

10

The finished dish with chopped parsley.

Scampi à la Boulevard
Boulevard Scampi

One cover

◆ Ingredients

150 g (6 oz) of jumbo scampi rolled in flour
25 g (1 oz) butter
12 ml (½ fl oz) oil
100 ml (3½ fl oz) double cream
1 measure dry vermouth
1 measure brandy
Salt and pepper
1 portion hot pilaff rice and yellow peppers (to be brought in from the kitchen when the dish is ready)

◆ Equipment

1 flare lamp
1 suzette pan
2 service spoons and forks
2 cold joint plates for the cutlery and to rest the pan on
1 hot fish plate
1 clean serviette

Season the floured scampi and heat the butter and oil.

Place the scampi in the suzette pan and sauté quickly.

When the scampi are cooked, add a measure of dry vermouth and reduce by half.

Flame with brandy.

Add the double cream and reduce.

The completed dish with pilaff rice.

Scampi au Pernod
Scampi with Pernod

One cover

Note: Season the scampi and sauté as for Scampi Boulevard.

◆ Ingredients

150 g (6 oz) jumbo scampi rolled in flour
25 g (1 oz) butter
100 ml ($3\frac{1}{2}$ fl oz) double cream
2 measures Pernod
Salt and cayenne pepper
1 portion hot pilaff rice (to be brought in from the kitchen when the dish is cooked)

◆ Equipment

1 flare lamp
1 suzette pan
2 service spoons and forks
2 cold joint plates for the cutlery and to rest the pan on
1 hot fish plate
1 clean serviette

Add the Pernod.

Flame.

Add the double cream and reduce slightly.

Serve the scampi on a bed of pilaff rice.

Dust with cayenne pepper.

Steak Diane
Steak Diane

One cover

◆ Ingredients

1 × 225 g (8 oz) sirloin
   steak trimmed of fat and
   batted out very thin
French mustard
Worcester sauce
25 g (1 oz) butter
25 g (1 oz) chopped onions
25 g (1 oz) sliced mushrooms
75 ml (2 fl oz) red wine
1 measure brandy
100 ml ($3\frac{1}{2}$ fl oz) sauce demi-glace
Salt and pepper
Chopped parsley

◆ Equipment

1 flare lamp
1 suzette pan
2 service spoons and forks
2 cold joint plates for the
   cutlery and to rest the pan on
1 hot joint plate
1 clean serviette

2

Season the sirloin steak.

3

Coat the steak lightly with French mustard.

4

Roll the steak on to a service fork.

5

Heat the butter in the suzette pan and when hot, unroll the steak into the pan taking care to do it away from the customer.

6

Add a dash of Worcester sauce.

7

Turn the steak and cook on the other side.

8

Remove the steak from the pan and place it on a hot fish plate. Cover with a second plate to keep hot.

9

Sauté the onions and mushrooms in the pan (add a little more butter if required).

10

Return the steak to the pan.

11

Add the red wine and reduce.

12

Add the sauce demi-glace.

13

Flame with brandy.

14

Serve the sirloin steak on a hot joint plate and garnish with a little chopped parsley.

◆ Monkey Gland Steak ◆

One cover

1

▶ Ingredients

1 × 225 g (8 oz) fillet steak
  batted out very thin
Dijon mustard
Worcester sauce
25 g (1 oz) butter
25 g (1 oz) chopped onions
25 g (1 oz) sliced mushrooms
1 measure brandy
$\frac{1}{2}$ measure dry Madeira
100 ml ($3\frac{1}{2}$ fl oz) sauce demi-glace
Salt and pepper
Chopped parsley
75 ml (2 fl oz) double cream

◆ Equipment

1 flare lamp
1 suzette pan
2 service spoons and forks
2 cold joint plates for the
  cutlery and to rest the
  pan on
1 hot joint plate
1 clean serviette

2

Season the fillet steak.

3

Spread the steak with Dijon mustard.

4

Roll the steak on to a service fork.

5

Heat the butter in the pan. Unroll the steak and cook on one side.

6

Add a dash of Worcester sauce.

7

Turn the steak over and cook on other side.

8

When cooked, remove and place between two hot fish plates.

9

Cook the mushrooms and onion (add a little more butter if necessary).

10

Drain the juices from the steak into the pan.

11

Return the steak to the pan. Add the Madeira and deglaze the pan.

12

Add the measure of brandy and flame.

13

Add the sauce demi-glace.

14

Add the double cream and reduce.

15

Serve on a hot joint plate and finish with chopped parsley.

Filet de Boeuf à la Stroganoff
Fillet of Beef Stroganoff

One cover

◆ Ingredients

1 × 225 g (8 oz) fillet steak cut
  into batons
Olive oil
25 g (1 oz) chopped onions
25 g (1 oz) sliced mushrooms
5 g ($\frac{1}{6}$ oz) paprika
100 ml ($3\frac{1}{2}$ fl oz) sauce demi-glace
100 ml ($3\frac{1}{2}$ fl oz) sour cream
1 measure brandy
Salt and pepper
Chopped parsley
1 portion hot pilaff rice (to be
  brought in from the kitchen
  when the dish is cooked)

◆ Equipment

1 flare lamp
1 suzette pan
2 service spoons and forks
2 cold joint plates for the
  cutlery and to rest the
  pan on
1 hot joint plate
1 clean serviette

Add the oil to the suzette pan
and heat until it is hot.

Add the strips of fillet steak.

Season.

Add paprika.

Add the chopped onions and
cook for approximately 1
minute.

Add the sliced mushrooms and
finish cooking.

8

Add the measure of brandy and flame.

9

Add the sauce demi-glace.

10

Finish with sour cream. Reduce slightly.

11

Position the pilaff rice on a hot joint plate.

12

Make a well and place the steak into the centre.

13

The finished dish.

Piccata al Marsala
Veal Medallions in Marsala Wine

One cover

◆ Ingredients

4 × 50 g (2 oz) very thin veal
  medallions rolled in flour
25 g (1 oz) butter
100 ml (3½ fl oz) sauce demi-glace
1 measure Marsala wine
1 measure brandy
Salt and pepper
Chopped parsley

◆ Equipment

1 flare lamp
1 suzette pan
2 service spoons and forks
2 cold joint plates for the
  cutlery and to rest the
  pan on
1 hot joint plate
1 clean serviette

Place the butter in the pan and heat until it is hot.

Place the floured veal into the suzette pan.

Season with salt and pepper.

Turn the veal over in the pan and cook the other side.

Add the Marsala wine and deglaze the pan.

Add the measure of brandy and flame.

92

8

Add the sauce demi-glace.

9

Serve on a hot joint plate.

10

The finished dish with chopped parsley.

One cover

◆ Ingredients

1 × 225 g (8 oz) fillet steak cut in two medallions
   and coated with crushed black peppercorns
25 (1 oz) butter
Olive oil
Salt
100 ml ($3\frac{1}{2}$ fl oz) double cream
1 measure brandy

◆ Equipment

1 flare lamp
1 sauteuse pan
2 service spoons and forks
2 cold joint plates for the cutlery and to rest the
   pan on
1 clean serviette

Add the butter and oil to the sauteuse and heat
until they are hot.

Place the fillet steak into the pan.

Season with salt.

When cooked on one side, turn the steak over
and cook the other side.

6

Flame with brandy.

7

Add the double cream.

8

Place the steak on to a hot joint plate.

9

Reduce the cream and coat the steak with the sauce.

10

The finished dish.

◆ Rognons d'Agneau Flambés ◆
Flamed Lambs' Kidneys

One cover

◆ Ingredients

225 g (8 oz) lambs' kidneys cut into halves
25 g (1 oz) butter
Olive oil
25 g (1 oz) chopped onions
25 g (1 oz) sliced mushrooms
$\frac{1}{2}$ measure Madeira
1 measure brandy
100 ml ($3\frac{1}{2}$ fl oz) sauce demi-glace
100 ml ($3\frac{1}{2}$ fl oz) double cream
Salt and pepper
Chopped parsley

◆ Equipment

1 flare lamp
1 suzette pan
2 service spoons and forks
2 cold joint plates for the cutlery and to rest the pan on
2 hot joint plates
1 clean serviette
1 hot flat to keep the kidneys warm

2

Place the butter and oil in the pan and heat until it is hot.

3

When the butter and oil is ready, add the kidneys and sauté quickly on one side.

4

Season with milled pepper and salt.

5

Turn the kidneys over and sauté on other side.

6

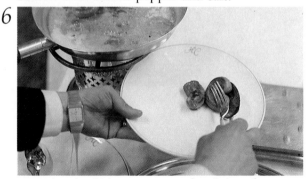

Transfer the kidneys on to a hot joint plate.

7

Cover with another hot joint plate and place on a hot plate.

8

Add the chopped onions and the sliced mushrooms.

9

Season to taste.

10

When the vegetables are cooked, return the kidneys to the pan.
Note: Do not serve the juice which has drained from the kidneys because it could cause the sauce to become bitter.

11

Deglaze the pan with the Madeira.

12

Flame with the measure of brandy.

13

Add the double cream and reduce.

14

Arrange the kidneys on to a hot joint plate. Coat with the sauce.

15

Sprinkle with chopped parsley.

Crêpes Suzette
Pancakes Suzette

Two covers

◆ Ingredients

4 thin pancakes
25 g (1 oz) castor sugar
8 sugar cubes rubbed on
   the skin of an orange
1 lemon
25 g (1 oz) butter
100 ml ($3\frac{1}{2}$ fl oz) orange juice
50 ml ($1\frac{3}{4}$ fl oz) lemon juice
1 measure Grand Marnier
1 measure brandy

◆ Equipment

1 flare lamp
1 suzette pan
2 service spoons and forks
2 joint plates for the cutlery
2 hot sweet plates
1 clean serviette

Cover the centre of the suzette pan with a layer of sugar and allow it to caramelize.

When golden brown, add the butter.

Mix well using the lemon wedge on the end of the fork. The lemon adds flavour and it prevents the pan from being scratched.

Add the orange juice.

Add the lemon juice.

Mix well with the end of the lemon.

8

Add the sugar cubes and allow the cubes to soften in the liquid before crushing them with the end of the lemon.

9

Turn down the flame and, without flaming, add the Grand Marnier.

10

Blend the liquids together and allow the sauce to reduce. Test the consistency by dragging the end of the lemon across the pan. When the sauce becomes transparent it is ready.

11

Roll the pancakes singly on to a service fork. Unroll them into the pan.

12

Turn the pancakes over to ensure that they are coated with the sauce.

13

Fold the pancakes into quarters and arrange them neatly in the centre of the pan.

14

Add the brandy and flame. Sprinkle with castor sugar, while flaming, for effect.

The finished dish.

Banane Flambée au Rhum
Banana Flamed with Rum

One cover

◆ Ingredients

1 firm banana
25 g (1 oz) butter
25 g (1 oz) castor sugar
50 ml (1¾ fl oz) orange juice
1 measure dark rum
1 scoop of vanilla ice cream
(to be brought in from the
kitchen when the dish
is cooked)

◆ Equipment

1 flare lamp
1 suzette pan
2 service spoons and forks
1 × 100 mm (4 oz) paring knife
3 joint plates for peeling the
banana, for the cutlery
and to rest the pan on
1 clean serviette
1 hot sweet plate

Method 1

2

Using a service spoon and fork lift the banana on to a clean serviette.

3

Grip the end of the banana between the thumb and paring knife. Cut off the end, taking care not to cut completely through the skin. Pull back the skin and peel along the length of the banana.

4

Turn the banana and repeat the operation with other end.

5

Peel the remaining two strips using thumb and paring knife.

6

Place the peeled banana on a clean 200 mm (8 in) plate and cut as illustrated.

Method 2

Place the banana on 200 mm (8 in) plate. Using a sharp paring knife, trim the ends of the banana.

Using a service spoon and fork lift the banana on to a clean serviette.

Cut the banana in half, lengthways, taking care not to use excessive pressure.

Place the two halves on to a clean 200 mm (8 in) plate and remove the skin using a service spoon and fork.

The banana is ready for cooking. *Note*: Whichever preparation technique is used, the method of cooking is the same.

Place the butter in the pan and heat until it is hot.

Sauté the banana slices quickly.

Sprinkle liberally with castor sugar.

15

Turn the banana slices over.

16

Sprinkle again with castor sugar and allow to caramelize.

17

Add the orange juice.

18

Allow the orange juice to blend and dissolve the caramel. Reduce slightly.

19

Add the dark rum and flame. Sprinkle with castor sugar, while flaming, for effect.

20

Serve on a hot 200 mm (8 in) plate with vanilla ice cream.

Pêches Flambées au Cognac
Peaches Flamed with Cognac

Two covers

◆ *Ingredients*

6 half peaches in syrup
25 g (1 oz) butter
25 g (1 oz) castor sugar
2 measures Cognac
2 scoops of vanilla ice cream
(to be brought in from the
kitchen when the dish is
cooked)

◆ *Equipment*

1 flare lamp
1 suzette pan
2 service spoons and forks
2 joint plates for the cutlery
and to rest the pan on
1 clean serviette
2 hot sweet plates

Cover the centre of the suzette pan with a layer
of castor sugar. Allow the sugar to caramelize.

Add the butter and blend in.

Add the peaches and a little of the peach syrup.

Heat the peaches and allow the sauce to reduce.

Flame with Cognac.

Serve on a hot 200 mm (8 in) plate with vanilla
ice cream.

Ananas Flambé au Kirsch
Pineapple Flamed with Kirsch

Two covers

Note: The pineapple has been peeled and sliced before commencing this operation. See preparation of fresh pineapple on page 126.

◆ *Ingredients*

2 slices of fresh pineapple
25 g (1 oz) butter
25 g (1 oz) castor sugar
50 ml (1¾ fl oz) orange juice
2 measures Kirsch
2 scoops of vanilla ice cream (to be brought in from the kitchen when the dish is cooked)

◆ *Equipment*

1 flare lamp
1 suzette pan
2 service spoons and forks
2 joint plates for the cutlery
4 clean serviettes
2 hot sweet plates

Cover the bottom of the suzette pan with castor sugar. Allow the sugar to caramelize.

Add the butter and blend.

Place the slices of pineapple into the pan and cook.

Add the orange juice.

Turn the pineapple over and cook on the other side.

Add the Kirsch. Note how the pan has been pulled back to allow the flame to ignite the vapours.

Flame and sprinkle with castor sugar for effect.

9

Place the cooked slices on to a hot 200 mm (8 in) plate.

10

Coat the slices with the sauce.

11

Place a scoop of ice cream into the centre of the pineapple.

12

The finished dish.

◆ Zabaglione ◆

Two covers

◆ *Ingredients*

4 eggs
25 g (1 oz) castor sugar
2 measures Marsala wine
Ground cinnamon
4 biscuits à la cuillère

◆ *Equipment*

1 flare lamp	1 glass dish for the debris
1 silver bowl	2 glass coupes on
1 egg whisk	underplates with doileys
1 soup ladle	1 clean serviette

Break the eggs and separate the yolks from the whites.

Place the yolks into the bowl.

Add castor sugar.

Add the Marsala wine.

Blend together with a whisk.

Cook on a flare lamp and whisk continuously. Take care not to over cook.

8

When the mixture reaches ribbon stage it is ready.

9

Portion the mixture into the glass coupe using a ladle.

10

Finish the dish by sprinkling with ground cinnamon. Serve on 200 mm (8 in) doileyed plate with biscuits and a teaspoon.

Cerises Jubilé
◆ Cherries Flamed with Kirsch ◆

One cover

◆ *Ingredients*

24 black cherries in syrup
25 g (1 oz) sugar
1 measure Kirsch or cherry Brandy
1 scoop of vanilla ice cream (to be brought in from the kitchen when the dish is cooked)

◆ *Equipment*

1 flare lamp
1 suzette pan
2 service spoons and forks
2 joint plates for the cutlery and to rest the pan on
1 clean serviette
1 hot sweet plate

Caramelize the sugar.

Add the cherries and syrup.

Heat through and reduce the sauce.

Add the Kirsch and flame.

Serve on a hot 200 mm (8 in) plate with vanilla ice cream.

The finished product.

Two covers

1

◆ Ingredients

1 450 g (16 oz) sirloin steak
Béarnaise sauce
Garnishes

◆ Equipment

1 × 150 mm (6 in) stainless steel knife
1 hot service plate for carving
2 hot joint plates
1 service spoon and fork
1 clean serviette

Method one

2

Transfer the sirloin steak on to a hot joint plate. Hold it steady with the fork (do not pierce the joint with the fork). Commence carving, holding the knife at an angle of approximately 45 degrees.

3

Carve 6 mm ($\frac{1}{4}$ in) slices of steak. Rearrange on the hot flat and serve with béarnaise sauce and garnishes.

Method two

4

After trimming the excess fat, cut the sirloin steak into two equal portions.

5

Once portioned, transfer to a hot flat. Serve as for method one.

Two covers

◆ *Ingredients*

1 450 g (16 oz) fillet steak

◆ *Equipment*

1 × 150 mm (6 in) stainless steel knife
1 hot service plate for carving
2 hot joint plates
1 service spoon and fork
1 clean serviette

1

2

Fillet steak ready for presentation.

3

Push the carving knife under the fillet steak and hold it steady with a service fork, taking care not to pierce the meat. Transfer on to a hot joint plate.

4

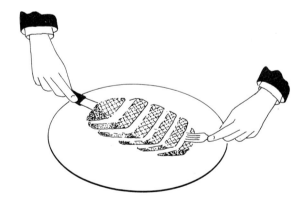

Hold the steak down with the fork and begin slicing at an angle across the grain of the meat.

5

Cut the steak into approximately six slices of equal thickness. Transfer the slices on to a hot flat. Serve according to customer preference, i.e. the rarer cuts would come from the centre.

Selle d'Agneau ◆
Saddle of Lamb

One cover

1

The saddle of lamb ready for presentation.

◆ *Ingredients*

1 saddle of lamb

◆ *Equipment*

1 large carving board
1 × 150 mm (6 in) stainless steel knife
1 plate for the debris
1 service spoon and fork
1 hot flat to keep the carved meat warm
1 clean serviette

2

Make an incision lengthways along either side of the backbone.

3

Make incisions in the flesh through to the bone, approximately 12 mm ($\frac{1}{2}$ in) wide on both sides of the backbone down to the skirting of fat.

4

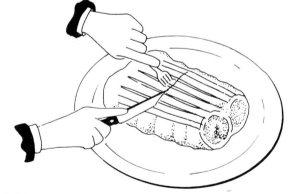

Make an incision across the full width of the saddle.

5

Prise the fillets of lamb free from the bone using a service spoon.

6

Arrange the fillets neatly on a hot flat.

7

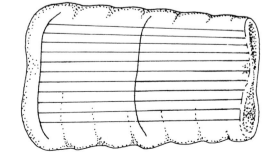

How to cut a saddle of lamb.

Two covers

Ingredients

1 best end of lamb

Equipment

1 × 150 mm (6 in) stainless steel knife
1 hot service plate for carving
2 hot joint plates
1 service spoon and fork
1 clean serviette

1

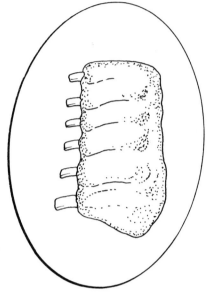

Best end of lamb ready for presentation.

2

Insert a service fork between the ribs and lift the lamb on to a hot joint plate. Do not pierce the eye of the meat.

3

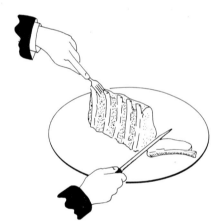

Hold the lamb upright with a service fork and start carving from the opposite end to that held by the fork.

4

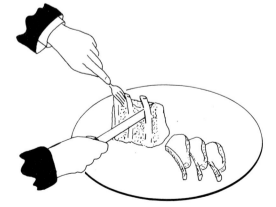

Portion into cutlets of equal size.

5

Rearrange the cutlets neatly on the flat and ensure they are hot. Serve on a hot joint plate with appropriate accompaniments.

Two covers

1

Transfer the saddle of hare on to a hot joint plate.

◆ *Ingredients*

1 saddle of hare

◆ *Equipment*

1 carving board
1 × 150 mm (6 in) stainless steel knife
1 service spoon and fork
1 hot flat to keep carved meat
1 clean serviette

2

Hold the saddle firmly on the joint plate with the service fork resting on the backbone. Push the service spoon down between the fillet and the backbone.

3

Prise the fillet away.

4

Repeat the operation with the other side.

5

Hold the knife at an angle and cut each fillet into approximately four slices.

Poulet Rôti
◆ Roast Chicken ◆

Four covers

◆ **Ingredients**

1 large roast chicken

◆ **Equipment**

1 × 150 mm (6 in) stainless steel knife
1 hot service plate for carving
1 service spoon and fork
4 hot joint plates

1

The chicken ready for presentation.

2

After draining the chicken transfer it on to a hot joint and remove the winglets. Place them on a debris plate.

3

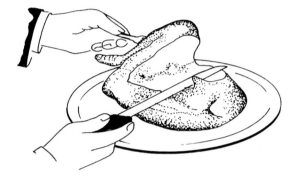

Turn the chicken on its side and remove the leg.

4

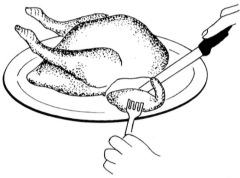

Cut the leg into two. Repeat the operation with the other leg. Transfer the cut pieces on to the hot flat.

5

Hold the chicken steady by inserting a service fork into the base of the carcass and detach the parson's nose but retain skin.

6

Portion one half of the breast into two and cut down through the wing bone joint. Using the breast bone as a guide, slice off the remaining portion of breast. Repeat the operation with the other half of breast.

7

Serve a piece of dark meat with a piece of white meat. The portions should be thigh with wing piece, and drumstick with long piece of breast.

Caneton Rôti
◆ *Roast Duckling* ◆

Two covers

1

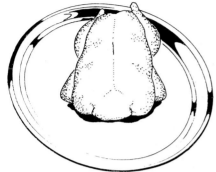

The duckling ready for presentation.

◆ *Ingredients*

1 medium sized duckling

◆ *Equipment*

1 × 150 mm (6 in) stainless steel knife
1 hot service plate for carving
1 service spoon and fork
2 hot joint plates

2

After presentation, insert the knife into the neck of the bird and the fork between the thigh and the drumstick. The duckling should be lifted and drained of the juices, and transferred on to a hot joint plate.

3

Turn the duckling on to its side. Prise the leg away from the carcass using a service fork. Cut any retaining flesh with the knife. Repeat the operation with the other side.

4

Hold the duckling steady by inserting the service fork at the base of the carcass. Make an incision along the length of the breastbone on both sides. Remove the breast from one side and transfer it on to a hot flat.

5

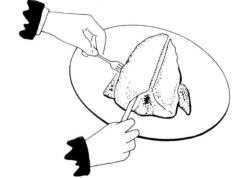

Repeat with the other breast.

6

Serve one breast per portion. The legs should be returned to the kitchen and used for making pâté or bortsch.

Grouse Rôtie ◆
Roast Grouse

One cover

1

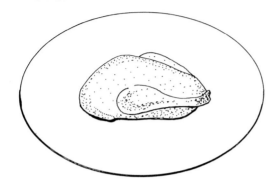

◆ *Ingredients*

1 young grouse

Note: A large grouse can be served for two covers.

◆ *Equipment*

1 × 150 mm (6 in) stainless steel knife
1 hot service plate for carving
1 service spoon and fork
1 hot joint plate

2

After presentation, insert the service fork firmly into the grouse. Lift it, drain any juices and, with the help of a knife, place it on to a hot joint plate.

3

Turn the grouse upright and commence carving from the tail end.

4

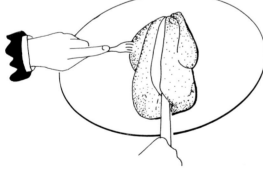

Carve the grouse through the breastbone into two halves.

5

Remove the backbone.

6

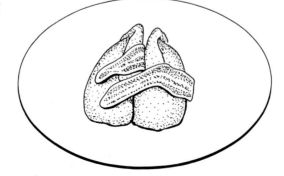

Serve the two halves or one half per portion, depending on the size of the grouse.

Faisan Rôti
Roast Pheasant

Two covers

1

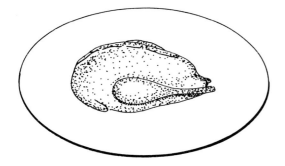

◆ *Ingredients*

1 medium-sized pheasant

◆ *Equipment*

1 × 150 mm (6 in) stainless steel knife
1 hot service plate for carving
1 service spoon and fork
2 hot joint plates

2

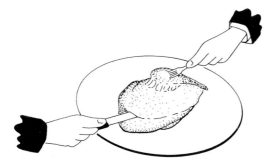

Present the pheasant, lift it and drain off the juices. Transfer the pheasant on to a hot joint plate. Remove the legs. The legs should be returned to the kitchen and used in the preparation of other game dishes.

3

Turn the pheasant upright, insert the fork into the base of the carcass. Hold it steady and score the breasts. The scoring of the breasts is done to allow the roast gravy to moisten the flesh as a pheasant can sometimes be dry.

4

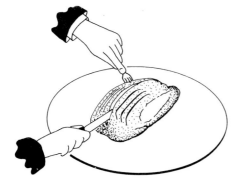

Carve the breasts.

5

Use the fork to help separate the breasts from the carcass.

6

Place the breasts on to the hot flat and serve one breast per portion.

◆ *Cánard Sauvage à la Presse* ◆
Pressed Wild Duck

Two covers

◆ Ingredients

1 × 1.25 kg (2½ lb) wild duck,
  lightly roasted
(approx. 20 minutes)
1 glass of good red wine
1 glass of port
Rind of 1 lemon
6 pepper-corns
Salt and pepper
25 ml (1 fl oz) sauce demi-glace
Chopped parsley

◆ Equipment

1 duck press
1 service spoon and fork
1 × 150 mm (6 in) stainless
  steel knife
1 hot service plate for carving
1 flare lamp
1 suzette pan
1 rechaud
1 hot flat
1 plate for the debris

Place the suzette pan on the flare lamp and pour in a glass of good red wine.

Add the rind of one lemon.

Add the peppercorns and leave to reduce.

Insert the knife into the neck of the duck and transfer on to a hot joint plate.

Turn the duck on to its side.

Make an incision around both legs.

8

Make a shallow incision along the length of the breastbone.

9

Insert the service spoon under the skin and detach it from the flesh.

10

Repeat the operation on the other side and transfer the skin to a debris plate.

11

Insert the fork into the base of the duck and pin it down on the plate.

12

Proceed to carve very thin slices (aiguillettes) from the breast.

13

Push the slices away from the carcass using a service spoon.

14

Transfer the slices on to a very hot dish and place on to a rechaud.

15

Cut the carcass.

16

Remove the container from the duck press.

17

Place the chopped carcass into the container.

18

Press the carcass to extract any remaining blood.

19

Add the sauce demi-glace to the reduced red wine.

20

Add the port and reduce further.

21

Allow the pan to cool before adding the blood from the carcass.

22

Return the pan to the heat and season. Heat gently until the sauce thickens.

23

Coat the slices with the sauce. Sprinkle with chopped parsley.

One cover

1

◆ *Ingredients*

220 g (7 oz) finely
   chopped fillet steak
10 g ($\frac{1}{3}$ oz) chopped
   onions
2 anchovy fillets
5 g ($\frac{1}{6}$ oz) capers
5 g ($\frac{1}{6}$ oz) paprika
1 egg yolk

Olive oil
Worcester sauce
French mustard
Salt and pepper
$\frac{1}{6}$ measure brandy
Juice of $\frac{1}{4}$ lemon
Chopped parsley

◆ *Equipment*

2 service spoons and forks
2 joint plates
1 soup plate for mixing the steak

2

Start to make the sauce by putting the salt, pepper, and French mustard into the soup plate.

3

Add the lemon juice.

4

Combine the ingredients with a service fork.

5

Add a little olive oil.

6

Add the egg yolk and a little more olive oil. Mix well.

7

Ensure that an emulsion is achieved.

8

Add the dry ingredients and mix well.

9

Add the chopped steak and fold in the sauce using a service spoon and fork. The sauce should be evenly distributed through the steak.

10

Add a little brandy and mix well.

11

Transfer to a cold joint plate and shape with two forks.

12

Garnish with onion rings and chopped parsley. Anchovy fillets may be chopped and added with the dry ingredients, or kept whole and used to garnish the finished dish.

◆ *Oranges au Kirsch* ◆
Oranges with Kirsch

Two covers

1

◆ *Ingredients*

   2 firm oranges
   2 measures Kirsch
   Castor sugar

◆ *Equipment*

   1 × 100 mm (4 in) stainless steel paring knife
   2 service spoons and forks
   1 joint plate to peel the oranges
   2 sweet plates
   1 clean serviette

2

Transfer the orange on to a cold 200 mm (8 in) plate. Hold it steady with a service fork and cut off the end which was attached to the tree.

3

Turn the orange on to its cut end, pierce the cut piece with the service fork and push the fork into the centre of the orange.

4

Turn the orange on to its side and cut an incision around the base of the uncut end. Take care only to cut skin deep.

5

Holding the orange steady on the fork proceed to peel using a very sharp paring knife.

6

Peel the skin off in one long continuous strip.

7

Allow the peeled skin to collect on the cold plate.

8

Remove the fork and hold the orange steady by pushing down between the uncut end and the flesh. Proceed to cut into thin slices.

9

Different ways of presenting the finished orange.

Ananas au Kirsch
Pineapple with Kirsch

Two covers

◆ *Ingredients*

1 large, firm pineapple
2 measures Kirsch
Castor sugar
2 maraschino cherries

◆ *Equipment*

1 × 100 mm (4 in) stainless steel knife
1 × 150 mm (6 in) stainless steel knife
2 service spoons and forks
1 joint plate to cut the pineapple on
2 sweet plates
1 clean serviette

Grip the pineapple with a clean serviette and cut off the end.

Using a sharp 100 mm (4 in) paring knife peel off the skin until the required portion of flesh is exposed.

Remove the black dots in the pineapple using a sharp 100 mm (4 in) paring knife by cutting a V-shaped channel.

Remove the strip containing the black dots.

6

Slice the pineapple.

7

Place the slice of pineapple on to a clean 200 mm (8 in) plate. Pierce the core with a fork and cut it out using the point of the paring knife.

8

Decorate with a maraschino cherry and serve.

Fraises Romanoff ◆
Strawberries Romanoff

Two covers

◆ *Ingredients*

250 g (8 oz) strawberries soaked in port and 25 g (1 oz) of castor sugar
10 g ($\frac{1}{2}$ oz) castor sugar
200 ml (7 fl oz) double cream
Lemon juice
1 measure orange Curaçao
2 strawberries for decoration

◆ *Equipment*

3 service spoons and forks
1 large glass dish to whip the cream in
2 glass coupes on underplates with doileys

1

2

Pour the double cream into a glass bowl.

3

Sprinkle liberally with castor sugar.

4

Add the Curaçao.

5

Beat the cream using two service forks.

6

Add a little lemon juice.

7

Fold in until the cream thickens.

8

Place the marinated strawberries into glass coupes.

9

Top with the beaten cream.

10

Decorate with whole strawberries.

11

The finished product.

Café Irlandaise
Irish Coffee

One cover

◆ *Ingredients*

1 pot strong black coffee
Brown sugar
1 measure Irish Whiskey
50 ml (1¾ fl oz) double cream

◆ *Equipment*

1 flare lamp
1 tray with whiskey bottle measure, brown sugar
 basin, cream jug and 2 teaspoons
1 Paris goblet on an underplate with a doiley

Heat the glass over the flare
lamp by turning it round using
the stem.

Put the sugar into the glass.

Measure the whiskey into the glass.

Leave a teaspoon in the glass and add the
piping hot coffee.

6

Stir until all the sugar is dissolved.

7

Steady the liquid with the spoon. Allow the bowl of the spoon to rest on top of the coffee and push it gently against the side of the glass.

8

Pour the cream into the bowl of the spoon until it comes within approximately 6 mm ($\frac{1}{8}$ in) from the top of the glass. Do not rest the cream jug on the rim of the glass and do not pour too quickly.

9

Serve on a doileyed side plate.

Aiguillette   A thin slice cut from the breast of poultry.

Au bleu   Method of boiling live fish (especially trout).

Bain-marie   A double saucepan or container of hot water used for slow cooking or keeping food hot.

Béarnaise sauce   Sauce made from a reduction of vinegar, egg yolks and clarified butter.

Beurre maître d'hôtel   Parsley butter.

Beurre noisette   Butter cooked until it turns brown.

Bisque   Shellfish soup.

Burner   Element in a flare lamp which is set alight.

Carré   Part of a restaurant supervised by a head waiter.

Carré, d'agneau   Best end of lamb.

Carte, à la   Menu with individually priced dishes prepared to order.

Cayenne   A type of pepper made from ground chillies.

Chef de rang   Station waiter.

Chiffonade   Shredded lettuce.

Choke   Inedible centre of a globe artichoke.

Commis de rang   Apprentice waiter.

Commis de suite   Apprentice waiter.

Cover   Name given to the place setting. Also used to describe the number of customers sitting at a table.

Crêpe   Pancake.

Darne   A steak of round fish on the bone.

Débarasseur   A junior member of the restaurant staff.

Debris plate   A plate used to hold discarded items of food.

Déglacer   To swill out using wine or stock.

Demi-chef de rang   A waiter in line to promotion to chef de rang.

Demi-glace   Sauce made from equal quantities of espagnole and brown stock, and reduced by half.

Deportment   Posture of a member of the restaurant staff in front of the customer.

Directeur du restaurant   Restaurant manager.

Entrecôte   Steak cut from the boned sirloin.

Flambé dish   A dish cooked or finished at the table and set alight with spirits or liqueurs.

Flamber   To set a dish alight with spirits or liqueurs.

Flare lamp   Lamp used to cook or reheat dishes in the restaurant.

Granton   Brand name of carving knife.

Grid   Top of a flare lamp on which the pan is rested.

Guéridon   Round table with a central pedestal. Trolley used to serve food from. High class style of service.

Hollandaise sauce   Yellow sauce made from a reduction of vinegar, egg yolks and clarified butter.

Hors d'oeuvre   Menu term describing a first course. A selection of delicate salads, cured meats and fish.

Jambon   Ham.

Maître d'hôtel   Head waiter.

Marinade   To steep food in a pickling or seasoned liquid in order to tenderize and flavour it.

Mayonnaise   Cold sauce made from egg yolks, oil, vinegar, salt, pepper and English mustard.

Médaillon   A small, round cut of meat.

Meunière   Fish shallow fried in butter and finished with a little lemon juice.

Mise-en-place   Preparations carried out before service commences.

Napper   To coat or mask with sauce.

Naturelle, cuisine   A style of cookery which uses the natural flavours and colours of the ingredients.

Nouvelle, cuisine   New style of cookery which concentrates on colour, taste and presentation.

Paring knife   Small, thin bladed knife.

Piccata   Small escalope of veal.

Poivre, au   Peppered.

Prosciutto crudo   Italian cured ham.

Rang   Station in a restaurant.

Ravier   A rectangular porcelain dish.

Rechaud   A set of metal plates used to keep food hot when serving.

Remoulade   Mayonnaise-based sauce with the addition of capers, gherkins, anchovy essence and fines herbs.

Riz pilaff   Savoury or pilaff rice.

Romanoff   Royal Russian Family.

Sauter   To shallow fry.

Sauteuse   A copper pan with sloping sides.

Score, to   To make shallow incisions.

Sommelier   Wine waiter.

Suzette   Lady reputed to have given the name to crêpes suzette.

Suzette pan   Copper pan used to cook dishes in the restaurant.

Tartare   Mayonnaise-based sauce as for remoulade, but without the anchovy essence.

Tartare steak   Finely chopped fillet steak eaten raw.

Tronçon   A cut of flat fish on the bone.

Truffle   Fungi found underground. The best known black truffles come from Périgord. White truffles are found in Piedmont, Italy.